THE *Joy* OF
BEING STUCK ON PAUSE

THE *Joy* OF BEING STUCK ON PAUSE

*Godly Principles On Living Life
When God Says Wait*

DR. RAYFORD E. MALONE

The Joy of Being Stuck on Pause: Godly Principles for Living Life When God Says Wait
by Dr. Rayford E. Malone

Cover Design by Atinad Designs.

© Copyright 2015

SAINT PAUL PRESS, DALLAS, TEXAS

First Printing, 2015

All rights reserved. No part of this publication may be reproduced, stored in a retrieval system, or transmitted in any form or by any means, electronic, mechanical, photocopying, recording, or otherwise, without the prior permission of the copyright owner, except for brief quotations included in a review of the book.

ISBN-10: 0-9963241-9-4
ISBN-13: 978-0-9963241-9-9

Printed in the U.S.A.

To You My Unnamed Reader.

May His countenance smile down upon you and give you Peace.

Contents

Introduction 9

CHAPTER 1: *THE COUNTING PROCESS* *13*
    Begin With The Correct Formula 18
    Looking Through the Wrong Lenses 23
    Maintaining A Forward Focus 27
    Did He Say Joy? 30

CHAPTER 2: *WHAT ARE YOU WAITING FOR?* *39*
    Giving God What Matters Most 50
    Our Perception of God 56
    What's At The Door of Your Heart? 60
    Sometimes We Choose To Fail 65
    Who's That Knocking? Should I Let Them In? 67
    Yes To Savior, No To Lord 69

CHAPTER 3: *ENLIGHTED, BUT STILL IN THE DARK* *75*
    Just A Face In The Crowd 86
    An Audience With The Master 89
    The Problem With Little Faith 93
    The Blessing Of Great Faith 96

CHAPTER 4: *UH, JESUS? – I'M STUCK!* *107*
    Just In Case We Meet The Lord! 110
    Who Touched Me? 114
    It's Called A Right Relationship 115
    The Pressure Of Seeing Others Get Blessed! 120
    What Do You Mean "Thousands"? 125
    The Waiting Game 129

CHAPTER 5: *WALK WITH ME, LORD!* *137*
    Learn To Walk With God 141
    Why Trouble The Teacher, Anymore? 150
    The Ministry In The Message 153
    The Problem Of Having Two Opinions 156

CHAPTER 6: *THE CONCLUSION OF*
    THE MATTER *165*
    My Valley Of Dry Bones 170
    Press Play 178
    All It Takes Is A Word From the Lord 179

Conclusion 183
Decision for Christ 185
Contact Us 187
Also Available from Rayford Malone 189

Introduction

A few years ago I was watching a relatively unknown sprinter named Usain Bolt run in the Olympics. I had heard he was blazing fast and a tremendous athlete, so in anticipation of seeing him run I was hyped up and excited to see if he really was the real deal or not.

As I sat in my bedroom waiting for the gun to sound, I was on the edge of my seat, and as soon as it went off I immediately heard my daughter begin crying upstairs. I instantly knew this was not her normal cry. I grabbed my remote and hit *pause* because I didn't want to miss the race, and I ran upstairs to see what had happened to my child.

After spending a few seconds consoling my daughter, I began walking down the stairs only to hear the TV in the living room heralding the world record time of Usain Bolt. Instantly I felt crushed!

I missed it!

I could hear the TV in the living room as the announcers began singing accolades about how fast he ran, but then a light went off in my head! I remembered I had paused the TV in the bedroom! I held on to the glimmer of hope that no one changed the channel on the TV while I was away. When I walked into my room and saw that the Olympics was still on pause, I gave a little shout because I would get to see the sprint after all.

I picked up my trusty remote, pointed it at the TV, and hit play.

Nothing happened!

I did like most of us do. I looked at my remote as if I was willing it to work and I pressed **play** more forcefully this time. Again nothing happened. Next, I started shaking my remote to see if maybe my battery was weak, then I stretched out my arm and put all my force in my hands to press the play button, but still nothing happened.

Now by this time, I'm starting to get frustrated. I was getting agitated because I wanted to see the race in real time. Sure I could have watched the race in the living room, but that wasn't how I wanted to view it. I wanted it on my terms. I didn't want to watch the TV in the living room because I would have to *rewind* my DVR, and then hit play.

Now as I became more frustrated, I noticed God speaking to me. He asked, "*Ray, why are you mad?*" I replied, "*Lord, all I want to do is go forward. I want to watch this race. I am tired of being on Pause and the remote doesn't work. I, I, I, I.*"

Do you get the point?

In the living room life was going forward in real time, but while I was in the bedroom I was stuck on pause because of something I could not control. I felt that life was passing me by because there was something I really wanted to see but was unable.

Yes I did what I was expected to do! What father hears his child cry out and doesn't check on her? What good father turns a deaf ear to his child's pain and anguish? Not me, and prayerfully not you, but my *reward* for being a good dad was missing out on a piece of life, a piece of *history*.

While I was frustrated, singing my own praises to God, I began noticing the further and further away He seemed. It was as if we had a crystal clear conversation to begin with, but the more I fussed and moaned, the less I could hear His voice. Then it hit me!

I was slowing down my own progress. Although the TV was on pause I was also on pause with God, all because of my attitude and my desire.

The longer I moaned, wailed, and fussed about

my situation the more bleak I felt internally to the point I simply turned off the TV. Then it hit me that my complaining cost me the pleasure of enjoying Usain breaking the world record. So I sat in my bedroom upset and disconnected from everyone simply because I didn't have a little talk with Jesus.

Have you ever felt like this? Have you ever felt that God placed your life on Pause? Have you ever encountered a situation where the only way you can get out is to deal one on one with God? Do you feel as if an area of your life has been stopped by God and for whatever reason, no matter how hard you try, you just can't seem to get life started in that area again?

If this is you, this book will be a tremendous blessing to your life. This book is designed to provide you with wisdom to recognize areas where you are stuck on pause and it gives you various techniques as to how you can overcome these seasons through your daily walk with Christ. Pauses in life happen whether we desire them to or not, but instead of rejecting them if we learn to look at them through the eyes of Christ we can learn to rejoice through them.

CHAPTER 1

The Counting Process

Indeed we count them blessed who endure.
~James 5:11

*Life can only be understood backwards;
but it must be lived forwards.*
~Soren Kierkegaard

Do you *feel* like your life is on pause? Do you *feel* stuck? Trapped? Encapsulated into a tight situation and you can't see how to get yourself out of it? You've tried going forward, and maybe you've tried going backwards, but inevitably neither worked and you found yourself immobilized.

Do you feel as if you are spinning your wheels in pursuit of goals in life, but you notice the harder you try, the slower you move? Do you often think,

"*I'll enroll in college next semester,*" but ten years later next semester has never come? Do you always feel as if you're the bridesmaid but never the bride? Maybe you feel God has taken a sign and marked "discontinued" or "better luck next time" across your hopes and desires. Do you feel as if your marriage has been locked in an intermission for years as the musical interlude of life continues to play? Or maybe you feel as if your life is like a hovering plane in a permanent holding pattern whose fuel tank is dangerously empty. Simply put, being "stuck on pause" can be described in many ways, but when you get to the nuts and bolts of it, the words basically mean *you feel like life is passing you by.*

These are simple examples of what it feels like to be stuck on pause. You know that you are supposed to go forward in life, but for some reason, no matter how hard you try, you just can't seem to start moving.

For many of us this is what our "pauses in life" feel like. They make us feel hopeless. We feel as if God has called a "time-out" in our lives and we feel abandoned. By definition the word "pause" simply means, a *temporary* stop, rest, or cessation of progress.

But what do you do if your temporary break has turned into an extended vacation? What do you do when your temporary feels like it's become permanent? What do you do if you can't get off pause? Or better yet, what do you do if

God won't let you?

From the definition of the word pause we know it means *a temporary stop*. In concept, pauses were never designed to be eternal. However, sometimes it seems that some pauses in life last a few seconds, but others may last decades. I believe periodically throughout our lives God will place us in temporary holding patterns to give us time to deal with the issues in our lives. This could mean time to reflect, grow, and return to ministry with a renewed mind and purpose, or it could be to deal with our sins.

In either case God gives you time to deal with you.

So, why would God put us on pause? I believe He does this for three main reasons. First, God wants us to *reflect*. He will put us on pause to give us time to reflect over our life and to consider the things we are doing. This is His way of allowing us to spiritually judge ourselves to see if we are walking in the will of God. Second, God wants to *restore* us in some vital way. God will put us on pause to give us some time alone with Him. This is a time of re-gathering ourselves, our thoughts, ideas, and goals by allowing Him to refocus us towards our life's purpose. Third, God uses them to *restrain* us in our pursuit of life or in dealing with spiritually tough situations. Sometimes, we're just not ready to move forward in life, so God will protect us by putting us on pause to give us some extra time to mature so we are prepared for the mountains He has placed in our path.

When we look at our pauses through the eyes of God, we see he uses them to teach us *hidden* things about ourselves. Once we've learned our lesson or gotten into the proper position, He seeks to return us to "play" as quickly as possible. However, when we complain, moan, and wail against His commands, it causes us to remain on pause until we have learned that our complaining directly impacts our progress in God.

If you read the introduction to this book I wrote about one of my experiences of being on pause by God, and I can truly say I disliked every second of it.

However, once I had learned what God sought to teach me, I had a moment to reflect on my time in pause. As I pondered about why God allowed this to happen, I soon learned several *additional* lessons about myself and the benefits of being stuck on pause. First, I learned pauses are *Godly* because God wants me to see, or experience Him in a new way. Second, I learned pauses are *necessary* because God uses them to teach me to focus only on Him. Third, I learned pauses are *always difficult* to handle because God used my pause to get me to focus on killing my flesh.

So there's value in our pauses! We just have to learn to

see our pauses the right way. So how do we do this? We must learn to look at our pauses through God's eyes, not ours.

Let me ask you a question? *Do you know how important pauses are in our daily walk? Do you know how significant these moments are to our direction in life?* If you took a few minutes and really scrutinized your walk in Christ, do you think you would have a difficult task being honest and grading yourself? Do you think you would handle your challenges better if you slowed down and studied the best way to handle them? Now if you belong to the perfect crowd and you say, *"I'm a 100 because I do the best I can all the time,"* this book isn't for you! Perfect people need not apply!

This book is for the imperfect people who know they are no-where near perfect. This book is for those who struggle, wrestle, and compete with the world and *themselves* on a daily basis as they strive to live better lives in Christ.

So as you are sitting in a quiet place surmising your score, how do you calculate your number? How do you add up your score? How do you ascertain the ultimate value of your life? Well to do this we must know where to begin, and the process starts with the right formula.

Begin With The Correct Formula

Truth be told, I hate math. Coming from a family of highly intelligent people, I have to say from elementary all the way through college mathematics was my hardest subject. My mother holds a Master's Degree in education, and my father is an electrical engineer; so education was the order of the day around the Malone household. Out of all the subjects I must say math was my Achilles heel because *I was never patient enough to seek to understand the process.*

In our household when it came to scholastic achievement, my parents divided the workload according to their specialty. My mother would handle the reading and writing, but my father would handle the areas of math. In my feeble attempt to understand math I always maintained math should *at all times* be simple. Two plus two should always *equal* four. *See, simple.*

Many believe life *should* be simple; however, time and life itself teaches us it isn't. Life is a complex journey that must be viewed and assessed periodically instead of one large assessment with a pass or fail grade marked at the end. As we travel through life, we must *constantly* seek to change and sometimes challenge our focus to see our lives as God does. When we do this, we begin to understand our pauses are designed by God to help us maintain the right course instead of hindering our progression in life.

So we must learn to appreciate and use these spiritual time-outs for their intended purpose. This is simply an opportunity to catch our breath, refocus our strategy, and jump right back into the game of life.

I remember day after day sitting down with my dad and trying to understand math. I surmise that it was something like trying to sit down to dissect and understand life. I remember promising myself that *this time* I would get it right! *However, I learned my "this time" inevitably turned into a "next time" because I was never prepared to succeed.*

As I tried to rationalize problem after problem, I always found myself getting more and more upset. Since I couldn't understand the concept of the equation my reason would soon depart, and inevitably I always ended up upset, angry and defeated. Then one day my father said, "*Ray, you can solve any problem, but you must always begin with the right formula.*"

That's when the light bulb finally came on! *I needed to understand the formula. Ding! Ding! Ding!* If you don't know it, here's God's mathematical formula for your life. Your life plus your submission to God equals a successful and Godly life. *Now that is simple.*

Now some might shout and say, "*Preacher that's too easy! My life plus submission to God has hardly equaled a successful life, let alone a Godly life! I am struggling in every area, my faith has been shaken, and now you're telling me some rendition of "don't worry be happy?" That doesn't work for me, and there's no way you can prove it to me otherwise."*

Well let's count up the cost and see what God is saying to us.

The purpose of counting something is to ascertain it's worth or its *ultimate* value. It could be an object, time, or money, but at the *end* of the counting process we are seeking to place value upon an object.

Here's a short example to count the *worthiness* of our lives. If someone gave you a ten gallon bucket filled to the brim with coins and they promised to give you all the monies, but only if you counted the monies correctly, would you be in a rush to complete this task? *If you're like me you wouldn't! Considering the importance of the outcome and the value of the coins I'm sure you'd take your time and count correctly.*

In my mind, I can see myself following my parent's instructions when it came to counting a large amount of loose cash. First, I would have to clean out an open area. Second, I would get a blanket and spread it across the floor. Next, I would get some paper, pencils, and a calculator. Then, I would get the bucket and slowly pour the monies into the middle of the blanket in one heap. Finally, I would sit down, get comfortable and take my time counting up my "soon to be" treasure.

Now that's just *preparing* to count. When it comes to the actual counting process, I would first separate all the monies according to its kind. Meaning I would put pennies with pennies, nickels with nickels, dimes with dimes, etc. Then I would count up the total number of coins and multiply it by its value. Once I count and recount the numbers of coins to make sure I have the right total, I would then put all the coins back in the bucket.

Keep in mind, while many would be in a rush to complete this task, I would take my time. Why? Because when you count something of immense value, like vast treasure, it takes time, patience, and a watchful eye. No man gets ahead by counting treasure with a "hurry up" attitude. No. You need to sit down, relax, and go slow as you take pleasure in counting all the coins correctly.

When you rush you make mistakes, and that is the spirit of the enemy. He wants to get you in a "gotta get it now" mindset, and when we begin to rush we might as well throw in the towel because mistakes are bound to happen. So stay focused on the end result!

Sure it might take a long time to count the treasure, but the amount of time it takes is nothing compared to the joy you will receive when you claim the treasure as your own. *Remember this is your treasure you're counting, so enjoy it!* This is the same sentiment the Apostle Paul shared in Romans 8:18 when he said, *"For I consider that the sufferings of this present time are not worthy to be compared with the glory which shall be revealed in us."* Keep in mind the revealed "glory of God" is our treasure and reward as Children of God. Presently we haven't received this glory. However we shall receive it in our glorified bodies when our Savior comes back to receive us as His own. (John 14:3) With this verse in mind not only shall we *receive* this treasure, but we *are* this treasure to God.

So don't guess! This is your life you're counting! You have to be meticulous! With each counted coin your bucket becomes more valuable. Stay focused on the end result and count with joy!

One of your coins might have been you obtaining your college degree, or you marrying the right person. Those are positives that are easy to see. But what about the things that we would naturally perceive as negative? What about the death of your grandmother, or the loss of your scholarship in college? How about being abused by your first husband or being taken advantage of at a college frat party? Are these positives?

To the human eye when we think of things like this they often come with regret, shame, and fear. However, in God's eyes these things that we perceive through human intelligence as negative experiences can be used for a Godly purpose. In God's eyes these negatives when shared as a testimony are positive coins. When you share what God has done in your life or what He brought you through, they might come from a negative place but they are positive coins in your bucket of life.

Once again, in the eyesight of God everything we do in life contributes to our overall value. This means positive as well as negative experiences.

Looking Through the Wrong Lenses

When I struggled in math it wasn't because I didn't have the intellect or ability to understand the work. I failed because I was looking through the wrong lenses. Likewise, when it comes to assessing the value of our lives, many of us look through the wrong lens. We see much of our lives as negative experiences instead of positive. Many of us see our trials, tribulations, and tests as experiences that *diminish* us rather than add to us.

If we were to use the example of the bucket of money, we would view the positives of life as coins to be *added* to our total. However, the negatives would make us *withdraw* money from the bucket. Instead of thinking of negatives in life as *deposits* into our spiritual walk, we *naturally* think of them as spiritual *withdrawals* that diminish our purpose and walk in God. This is why many of us seek to hide our negatives. *We just don't want others to know we think we're operating at a deficit.*

However this is not how God sees it and we need to learn to see our lives through His eyes. In Jesus the experiences of life are neither positive nor negative. It's how we perceive them that make them positive or negative.

Now this is a hard truth to learn. Counting negatives or things that hurt us as positives can be very difficult. *Life is difficult when you are looking through the right lens.* But if you couple your negatives with a skewed vision of life, it doesn't matter what God blesses you with, you'll always have a distorted perspective of life.

I remember once while working with my father on my math homework we were dealing with negative numbers. Now I have to say dealing with positive numbers was very difficult for me, so wrestling with negative numbers was comparable to being boiled alive! After being tortured for thirty minutes or so my father said, *"Ray, negatives are always difficult to handle. So don't focus on the negative. Focus on the formula."*

When you focus on the formula of God it makes the negatives of life so much easier to handle.

Early in my ministry I met a strong woman of God who was a cancer survivor. Throughout the course of her life cancer had attacked her body three times, and each time God healed her from the deadly disease. One day after church she told me she didn't like having cancer one bit, but she was thankful for the experience. Being truly perplexed I asked why, and she said the experience she endured brought her closer to God than she could have ever imagined.

When we focus on the formula it means we're focusing on what God is striving to teach us through our negatives and not the negative experience itself.

Let me ask you a question? Why do people go to eye doctors? The short answer is because *"they desire to see correctly."* As we age our eyes go through a wide array of changes. During most of these changes we are unaware of them, but when things get *blurry and out of focus we make an appointment with the eye doctor.* Maybe we begin having a hard time reading, or visually things seem obscure and cloudy. In either case we go to the eye doctor so he can help us see correctly.

This is what many of us fail to do with God. We refuse to visit the doctor when our lives get out of focus. So to help us refocus God allows us to get stuck on pause.

When you visit the eye doctor one of the first things he does is dilate your eyes. This is done so the doctor can have a better view of the internal structure of your eyes; however, for many of us this is extremely uncomfortable. When our eyes are dilated, we become more sensitive to the light because they allow more light to pass through!

So, if you want to see things God's way, you have to follow three basic steps: Give Him room to dilute your spirit with the Holy Ghost. This means opening up your entire being to Him and giving Him 100% access to one of the most important areas of your life, your vision. Next, let Him penetrate your soul with His light by accepting His will and direction even if it is momentarily painful. Finally, let Him adjust your spiritual sight and correct your vision, thus giving Him the chance to teach you how to see life through His eyes.

Keep in mind this is a process. It is not a "one and done procedure." Every so often you will have to allow God to dilute your spirit so He can examine your soul. Yes, it will be uncomfortable, but letting Him change your vision is the only way you can see God's formula correctly.

Maintaining A Forward Focus

At the beginning of this chapter there is a quote by Soren Kierkegaard that says *Life can only be understood backwards; but it must be lived forwards.* When we deduce the meaning of this quote, it teaches us we should learn from our past but live for our future. Since we can't change the past, we accept it and the things it taught us by taking the knowledge and wisdom we gained from it and use it to our advantage in the future.

This is what it means to have a forward focus. A person with a forward focus isn't concerned about the past, their mistakes, or their issues. They are singularly focused on the future and the hope that it brings.

Remember, if we examine the process of life we know it only moves in one direction, forward. No matter what you have endured or survived in life, the process only goes one way. As an emotional being many of us often wish we could "turn back the hands of times," but ultimately that is REGRET talking. Regret is simply a fleshly desire that the devil uses to twist our thinking and destroy our pathway.

If what you encountered in your past was that great for you then God would have allowed you to keep it. If it's in your past, then that's where you should leave it. Past relationships, memories and fantasies are weights that must be destroyed for you to totally walk into the light of God.

When you read James 5:11 the author was counting the endurance of men and women of God in his day as they endured their daily trials. The writer sums up or counts their daily struggles and tribulations in this one brief statement of certifying their lives by saying *"we count them blessed who endure."*

Why were these people blessed? They were blessed because constant pain leads to spiritual perfection, while constant pleasure leads to spiritual pacification.

In Genesis 15:6 God counted the faith of Abraham and his faith *proved* that he was righteous. *And he believed in the Lord, and He counted it to him as righteousness.* (Genesis 15:6) *Do you think Abraham's life had any negatives?*

At the beginning of Abrams' walk with God his lie almost condemned his wife to be violated by a heathen king. (Genesis 12:13) He tried to intercede for God by having sex with Hagar. (Genesis 16:4) Once she became pregnant Hagar began mistreating Sarah, and that led to Abram having to disown his first born son Ishmael. His sin caused Abram to forsake his first son Ishmael for the son of promise, Isaac (Genesis 21:12).

So, yes it is safe to say that Abraham's life held many negatives, but when God counted his positives with his negatives, Abram was still found righteous.

When a person has a forward focus, they set their mind on things above and they begin to walk with Christ. When this happens a fierce *spiritual and mental* battle ensues. The desires of the flesh are at war with the desires of the Spirit, and the one you feed most will win. If you feed your flesh by drinking, having sex outside of marriage, and living like the world, your flesh will win the battle for your soul. However, if you feed your spirit by reading your Bible, praying and seeking God with a whole heart, and confessing that He is your Lord and Savior you will be saved.

This is not to say you will live a perfect life, because we are human. We're going to make mistakes along the way. We've already seen that Abraham's life was not perfect, but no matter how many times he fell he continued to get back up again and seek God through the positive as well as the negative issues of life. *This is why He was counted as righteous -he endured.* Psalms 24: 16 confirms this when we read, *"For a righteous man may fall seven times and rise again."*

I'm sure each time Abram sinned he felt the bitter sting of disappointment. With each humbling *and* embarrassing experience he grew closer to God. I'm sure he felt shame for lying about his wife being his sister. I know it pierced his heart as he was being chastised by a heathen king. I know it stung him greatly when his wife came to him crying over the treatment she received from Hagar and Ishmael's treatment of Isaac. I know it must have ripped his heart in two when he had to send his son away into the desert with Hagar at God's command. However, each time he picked himself up from the ground, he made sure his relationship was intact with God. He assessed his situation by learning what to do and what not to do, and then he continued on his path.

Did He Say Joy?

James 1:2 says, *"My brethren, count it all joy when you fall into various trials."* But what person really counts their trials as joy? Did Peter "count it all joy" when he walked on water one moment but began sinking the next? Did the disciples "count it all joy" when they were being battered, beaten, and bruised by those who wanted to crush their spirit and their fellowship? Did Paul count it all joy when he sat in a roman prison awaiting execution by being crucified?

No, and Yes! None of these situations felt good to their flesh in the moment they went through their torment, torture and pain, but all were joyful in their spirits afterward because it brought them closer to Christ!

Isn't that what we all want -to be closer to Jesus?

When you are focused on the formula you'll notice it's not at the beginning of the trial that we have the bulk of our issues. Usually it's in the middle of our trial that we begin to break down. It's in the "going through" that many of us lose our faith and hope. *This is why we have the knowledge of God in our spirits beforehand!* We can't wait until we are in the middle of the sea to figure out we're "up a creek without a paddle" because that's *when* the storm hits, and that's *where* it's the most violent. It always hits you when you are stuck in the middle.   (Matthew 14: 23-25) In the same light, we can't wait for the war to begin before we figure out, *"Oh I need to put on the armor of God."* Why? Because it's too late!

You have to be prepared for the battle beforehand. As my old pastor used to say when I came to church without my Bible, "Malone, where is your Bible? You can't slay a dragon without you sword!"

I submit to you that you'll never understand the joy of being stuck on pause *while* you are going through your trial. However if you keep on living, I promise you'll understand the joy of being stuck on pause *after* your trials and tribulations are over.

In Acts Chapter Five the disciples faced a trial that was in many ways as unstable as the trial the disciples endured in the middle of the sea. These men where sharing Christ to all who would listen, and as their efforts became known the religious elect that followed the Old Testament Law commanded them to never speak the gospel of Jesus Christ. Faced with a decision to follow men or Christ, they pressed forward by testifying of God's goodness and they were beaten for their actions.

Child of God do you feel beaten for sharing Christ? If you do, you aren't alone, but let's see how the disciples handled this moment where their lives where stuck on pause.

The Bible says in Acts 5: 40-42, *"And when they had called for the apostles and beaten them, they commanded that they should not speak in the name of Jesus, and let them go. So they departed from the presence of the council, rejoicing that they were counted worthy to suffer shame for His name. And daily in the temple, and in every house, they did not cease teaching and preaching Jesus as the Christ."*

Saints, these men show us the way! See they were beaten by the religious elect, and they were commanded to stop preaching in His name, but as soon as they got out of their presence the praise party began! These men were not shouting *"Praise God"* in the moment the lash was ripping the flesh from their backs. However, these men were shouting the moment they were freed from the confines of this awesome trial.

Child of God here is my word of encouragement for you, "Don't lose your faith in the "going through." I know it is hard and you feel like you can't make it another three steps, but don't lose heart! God is with you and you will make it to your destiny if you don't faint!

If you have to take one step for the Father, and a second step for the Son, and the third step for the Holy Ghost, then make your steps in Jesus Name! Hallelujah!

As I stated earlier, if you are like me you won't feel that these experiences are good for counting. Many of us want to stand before God in our righteousness as dazzling ministers of God; however, this is not the case. There will be times in all of our lives when we will taste the bitter defeat of missing the mark of God. It does not matter if you miss the mark by inches or a mile. All that matters is you broke your fellowship with God and you feel distance from God, so it hurts.

Whenever you run into a place in your life when God puts you on pause, your spiritual mind should register several truths about God and your situation. *First*, you should know there is a *reason* why *you are on pause. Second,* there's something God expects you to learn from the situation. *Third,* God also uses our trials to show us who we really are and what sins we are allowing to operate in our life.

I know it does not seem right or fair. Just knowing that we should be shouting and praising God in the middle of our painful experience simply doesn't seem to feel right. *However, we must stay focused because walking in the spirit has nothing to do with what we think, want, or desire.* It is solely about what God wants out of our lives.

James says we should count it "All Joy" when we fall because our slipping from grace inevitably brings us closer to God. If you have fallen in sin, understand that the slipping from grace shows there is an area of your life that is not *complete* in God. James instructs us that when we slip or fall we should be patient because God is trying to teach us something. He is trying to teach us the reason why we fell and that we should be patient with ourselves during these times because the trial is to make us complete in God. This is the goal of James 1:4 which says, *"But let patience have its perfect work, that you may be perfect and complete, lacking nothing."*

Like most people I am my worst critic. No matter how well I preach, or what I've done in ministry, I've always felt I could have done something better. Now this attribute helps me push a little farther, and strive to do a little more in ministry, and I believe that is a good thing. However, our enemy knows me and often times he strives to turn this strength into a weakness. He tries to use this as a doorway to make me feel shame and try to make me feel like a failure.

This is why I praise God for my wife! Sure, the enemy knows me. He knows the old unsaved Ray. But praise God our Father gave me a strong woman of God by my side that knows the new saved Ray!

Whenever I start to feel down or frustrated because of my skewed vision, Sister Brenda is always there to step right in. Spiritually speaking, somehow Sister Brenda can just "sense" when I am beating myself up. Now I don't know how she does it because most of time the expressions on my face are the same, but she can read my spirit like a book. Sometimes she doesn't need to see my face nor physically look at me to tell when I'm stuck on "pause," but I know what's coming when she says to me, *"Boy that mind of yours is running like a steam engine! I can see smoke coming out your ears!"*

Then she starts interceding for me by leading me through the mathematical counting process just as my father did all those years ago. *When she does this she's helping me to focus on the formula as she helps me to count my coins.* Usually she will begin and end with three basic questions. Although she asks the questions in different ways, the formula is always the same. She will say, *"Did you preach what God said?"* And my answer is, "Yes." Her second question is, *"Did you stop when God said stop?"* And my answer is, "Yes." Now her last question is always the kicker, *"Then why are you beating yourself up?"*

Now, let me ask why are you beating yourself up? You are on "pause" for a reason, and the goal of this book is to find out why and to get the heck off pause! So let's begin our *forward focus by looking inward and seeking the real reason God has placed you on pause.*

Study Guide

Chapter 1: The Counting Process

1. What areas of your life are you on pause? Have you written them down? Have you prayed about them? Keeping in mind that God puts us on pause to reflect, restore, and restrain us. What is He teaching you in these three modes of Godly operation? Write them down and discuss.

2. Keep in mind that pauses are godly, necessary, and always difficult. Do you see them as a hindrance or a blessing? If Godly submission is necessary in order to get off pause, what do you think is keeping you on pause? What area of your life are you withholding from God? Can you sit quietly and meditate on your character and see what is making your pauses so difficult to handle?

3. When you are dealing with the negatives of life, are you concentrating on the formula or the negative itself? Are you concentrating on the destination or your immediate situation? As you look at your pauses has chapter one begun to change your view? Are you able to see your pause and a benefit to your path instead of a hindrance?

4. When you have a Forward Focus you concentrate on your future and not your past. As things stand today what issues are you carrying that you know you need to let go? What weights are you carrying that you need to bury? Review Hebrews 12:1. What should you do with your weights? Compare and discuss.

5. Given that James says we should count it "All Joy," can you begin to see your pauses are designed to teach you to follow Christ more closely? With that in mind can you count your positive and negative experiences of life as joyful when you share your testimony knowing that your struggles have blessed someone else's life?

CHAPTER 2

What Are You Waiting For?

So it was, when Jesus returned, that the multitude welcomed Him, for they were all waiting for Him.
~Luke 8: 40

All things come to him who waits – provided he knows what he is waiting for.
~Woodrow T. Wilson

Psalms 27:14 says, *"Wait on the Lord; be of good courage, and He shall strengthen your heart; Wait, I say, on the Lord!"* However I submit to you if you've ever been stuck on pause, this is the last thing you want to hear. If your "pauses" have been anything like mine, you're probably pulling your hair out by the roots with veins popping out on the side of your neck screaming at this book, *"Preacher, I'm tired of being stuck on pause! I need to get unstuck now!'*

Please understand I know the feeling! Been there – Done that. It's one of the reasons I'm bald today.

When we're in the waiting process, *having patience to let God work it out for your good* can be very difficult. Just being on pause can bring about many negative emotions as you witness others breezing through the same spiritual mud-hole you are trapped in. Many of us understand that there will always be pauses in our lives and we naturally assume that one prayer to God will get us out of our mud-hole and moving forward toward our purpose. But what do we do when we pray and God leaves us in our mud-hole? What do we do when we put God on a time limit and we see the clock ticking in our spirits but we believe God isn't listening?

For many of us we lower our head, dig in, and try to force, or rather will our way out of our mud-hole which only makes it worse because we inevitably dig ourselves in deeper.

This is the danger of *prolonged* pauses! When you're on pause and you see yourself spinning your wheels over and over again while giving maximum effort, it can be crippling to your self-esteem and self-worth. However, when you add longevity to your pauses, the issue moves from being an external issue (how I see things, so I can get off pause) to being an internal struggle (I must be the problem and that is the reason why I'm stuck). *Whenever this happens the problems in our pause become compounded.*

Before I begin this chapter, please allow me to say there's nothing wrong with you. You're simply stuck. So don't make your spiritual situation worse by trying to "will" or "force" your way out. Just because you're dealing with a tough situation doesn't mean you're the issue. The problem isn't with you as a person, but rather with your perception towards your pause.

As a young boy my brother and I were often tasked to plow fields with one of our father's tractors. Often times we had to travel through muddy roads and low boggy areas in the woods, so getting stuck was a part of daily life. I remember many days of riding along on top of the tractor one second without a care in the world, and before I knew it–*mainly because I wasn't paying attention–Pow!* I would be stuck in a mud hole!

Most times I would become angry at myself for not seeing the mud hole. Then I would get angry at the mud-hole itself, and finally I would get mad at God for putting the mud-hole in my path. As my anger mounted, I did what came natural. I tried to force this five thousand pound tractor and its cargo out of the situation by gunning the engine and trying to force my way through. *That only made things worse.*

For humans it's natural for us to try to force our way out of things. We've been told almost since birth that we have the power within us to achieve and overcome any obstacle that's in our path. We've been taught as humans that we have the reason, power, intellect, and determination to subdue any challenge. *But we must remember this is in the natural realm, not the spiritual realm.* When we try to do what comes natural in a spiritual realm, we make things so much worse.

So how did my father teach me to get out of mud-holes? He taught me three main lessons. The first lesson was *don't panic*! As my father said one day, "*Ray, don't panic. Your negative emotions are only making it worse.*" This is why we *must* keep our focus on the positives of life. (Philippians 4: 8-9) As we discussed in Chapter 1, whenever we allow ourselves to become negative about situations, it never shortens our pauses. In all actuality it lengthens our time on pause, and it compounds the negative stressors in our lives. So for the next chapter I would like to begin laying a foundation to help remove some of these stressors by discussing the waiting process itself.

The second lesson was *"remain calm and assess your situation."* You *can* get out of some mud-holes just by paying attention to your surroundings. If God has you on pause there's a reason. Maybe he is waiting on you to wake up to a special revelation of the spirit? Or maybe He is blocking you from entering a "spiritual field" that *you* think you are ready for, but *He* knows you are not.

Keep in mind this happened to Paul in Romans 1:13 and 1st Thessalonians 2:18. Notice in both letters Paul spoke of a desire to visit these great cities, but "he was hindered" from traveling to them. For many of us this can be disheartening, but at the right time in the proper season God allowed Paul to travel to both cities to receive a harvest of souls for God.

So what is the point of this? Being delayed doesn't mean being denied. Sometimes God keeps us on pause because we simply are not ready to proceed.

The third lesson is the easiest to understand – *When you are truly stuck; all you can do is wait on the calvary to come!* There were many days when I was sent out by my father to fulfill a task and I became stuck to the point where I was immobilized. I mean the tractor would not budge! Since previous knowledge told me I couldn't get myself out of the situation, it was all I could do to wait patiently for him to come and rescue me. One thing I knew, sooner or later my father was going to come for me.

In this instance my natural father is like our Heavenly Father. He knows how long each assignment should take. He knows every planned destination and if you don't show up within a reasonable amount of time, He'll send out the calvary.

Back then my calvary was my natural father, but *now* my calvary is His son Jesus Christ. He is my Shepherd and His words tell us in Luke 15: 3-7 that He will search for and find every lost sheep.

If you ask what I did during this down time, it's simple. I waited. Sure the first few times I was stuck I did not wait patiently. But over time when I truly learned to trust my father, and I knew he would come for me, I learned to pay attention to the beauty around me.

This is why there's "joy" when you are stuck on pause. There's beauty surrounding you and you probably don't even know it!

For me there was beauty in sitting by a quiet creek and listening to the water as it cascaded gently over the creek bed. I also learned the sweetness of watching squirrels playing amongst the trees as the fall breeze whispered in the midst of their branches. I saw the glory of God's handiwork when I saw a herd of deer running through an open field praising God as they bounded and frolicked towards the woods. Yes, Child of God, there's joy and beauty on your pause, but you must learn to calm yourself to see it.

So let's refocus as we begin with the most important questions in this chapter. What are you waiting on? Are you waiting to get off pause or are you waiting on Christ?

Yes, both questions require YOU to wait; however one requires you to walk in a direction you want to go. The other requires you to walk in a direction GOD wants you to go.

Whenever we find ourselves stuck on pause the first thing that should register is the thought, *"Wait a second; I've been here before." There's one thing about being stuck on pause, the more you experience spiritual pauses the quicker you'll learn how to get past them.*

Here's an example from my personal life that taught me how to recognize my seasons of pause. If there is one place that every preacher desires *not* to go, it's Flunks-ville. Now understand Flunks-ville is not a physical place; it's a *spiritual pause* and it's where God sends you when you're out of His will.

Maybe you've sinned and you don't want to repent, maybe you've been given a spiritual assignment and you're running from the responsibility, or maybe God said for you to apologize to someone and you're not following His instructions. Either way, if you're in Flunks-ville you're there for a reason, and nine times out of ten you already know the why.

God doesn't send you to Flunks-ville because you've made a mistake. He sends you because you are in open rebellion.

In my life I have gone to Flunks-ville three times, and I can tell you it's the one place I never desire to visit. But it's not like we choose to go to Flunks-ville!

One second you're trucking along in life without a care in the world and the next you're in Flunks-ville, USA Population 1.

The first time I went to Flunks-ville I had barely been preaching three years and I thought I didn't need to prepare nor consecrate myself for the message God called me to preach. However, that particular Sunday morning I got up frantic, trying to pray, because I knew in my spirit I wasn't ready. Sure I had time to prepare, but I had other things that were more important to me at the time.

After arriving at the church later that morning, I was greeted by the pastor and I was led into the pulpit as the service commenced. All through the service my head was down and I scarily looked around. As the praise and worship settled down, the pastor stood to introduce me and that's when I heard the voice of God give me some great but terrifying news! He said, *"Turn to Isaiah 55: 6-7 and read the text."* Thankful that God was speaking to me I opened my Bible to Isaiah 55 and I instantly became sick when I saw the text. It said, *"Seek the* LORD *while He may be found, Call upon Him while He is near. Let the wicked forsake his way, the unrighteous man his thoughts; Let him return to the* LORD, *And He will have mercy on him; And to our God, for He will abundantly pardon."*

When I read these words I knew my face had turned

green, and I felt like someone had just punched me in the gut! Immediately I felt nauseous and all I wanted to do to complete the picture for the people of God was grab my stomach with my right hand, place my left hand over my mouth, give a couple of dry heaves, and run to the bathroom.

As the pastor said my name the church erupted in applause, and my mind immediately rolled back over the past few weeks as I saw all the leisure and wasted time I had at God's expense. I saw hour upon hour of TV time, gossip time, hanging with my friends time, but there was no God time. I knew I should have been preparing for the sermon, but I took a lackadaisical attitude towards God and I knew my punishment was to preach without the presence of God on me.

This was the first time I went to Flunks-ville. Since that time I've gone to Flunks-Ville a few more times, and now I am familiar with this oasis of spiritual dryness. Whenever God sends me there, I understand there's something He is trying to get me to see or acknowledge in my life.

So what's Flunks-ville? It's the place where God lets you do it all by yourself.

Here's the funny part! Like a small, and petty child I even tried to use God's Word against Him! In my selfishness I told God, *"But You said you'd never leave me or forsake me!"* Then God said the sweetest thing. He said, "Ray, *I'll never leave you or forsake you. But since you treated Me and My message so lightly you will preach without me today."*

After that the Heavens went into lockdown status. There was no anointing, no presence of God, no special touch from the Lord. The entire time I stood I kept thinking, *"God loves me so much He has to show up!"* About halfway through the sermon I knew that was just another lie I had told myself. My words never came together, my speech was broken, my style and structure were off, and I must say I was so messed up I knew they would never invite me back.

So like any beaten child, after the service I made it my purpose to high-tail it out of there as soon as possible. On my way home I didn't call anyone. I did not want to talk to anyone. Nor did I want to be around anyone. It wasn't until years later that I finally realized what I was doing on that drive home.

I was waiting on God to come back. I was waiting for God to speak to me. I was waiting to feel His presence again. So mile after mile, town after town, I waited. *I knew it wasn't going to do me any good to talk to someone else about what God had done in my life because I knew the only One who could get me off pause was God Himself.*

When that revelation finally hit me, that was

the moment I opened my heart to God and I said, "*Father forgive me, I was wrong. I will never treat You or Your word lightly again.*" As I finished that prayer the spirit of God began to talk to me, and He said, "*So, how do you like Flunks-ville?*"

In that moment I learned a very important truth about God. *I learned that the anointing He has placed on my life is great, but it means absolutely nothing without a right relationship with God.* It was in that second that I felt just like the multitude in Luke 8:40; I was waiting eagerly for my true hope to show up.

Sure they stood on the shore and I was driving in my car, but in that moment of revelation we were on one accord. We were all waiting on Jesus.

The realization of the value of my relationship with God *before* I went to Flunks-ville is the same value many of us place on God *before* we are stuck on pause. We take it lightly. However, the value we place on God after we have experienced the longevity of a season of pause teaches us that He and our relationship with Him are truly invaluable.

See, negative experiences can add positive coins to your bucket!

Even though I had royally screwed up and I knew I needed God desperately, He did not show up until I began calling on His name in the car, *with the right attitude.* When I began uttering His name my spirit began ministering to me by saying, *"This is what it means to wait on the Lord and be of God courage. You know He loves you but you had to endure this season of pause to teach you to draw closer to Him."*

The true revelation of my pause unfolded before me as I drove home. I began to understand that the whole time I thought I was waiting on God; He was actually waiting on me! Praise God. If you're currently on pause, please understand you are not coming off pause until you have reestablished a right relationship with God.

In that moment my frown was turned upside down. I began praising God because I could see the lesson He was teaching me, and while I drove home He and I had a great conversation about how to stay out of Flunks-ville.

Here is a rule I have learned about coming off my pauses with God. If you complain –you will remain. If you praise –you'll be raised.

Giving God What Matters Most

Have you ever thought about what matters most to God? I have. A few years ago I read a book titled *The Five Love Languages,* and in essence this book taught me that men and women give and receive love differently. Some might believe showing love is in giving gifts. Others believe words of affirmation show love. Or one might receive love through physical touch like massages or foot rubs.

When it comes to giving and receiving God is no different from the rest of us. He has given us His best gift, His Son, and what have we given Him? What have we given in return?

Here is an example.

It's your birthday! It is your one special day out of the year, and you have a younger brother that was born on the same day. In searching to buy a present for your sibling you look for something that is as special and unique as your relationship. So you spend months looking for just the right gift, and one day you find it, wrap it, and put a bow on it for your sibling.

Well the big day arrives and you come to your brother and you present him with the best gift you had to offer. You sweated, toiled and found the perfect gift and you see the surprise, elation, and shock on his face as he opens the gift.

As you stand to receive your gift, you know beyond a shadow of a doubt that he has a great present for you as well. You know his dedication and love for you is no less than your love for him. As he extends your present you see in his hand a three cent bubble gum piece in a faded wrapper!

To top it off he gives you a brief hug and then

begins showing all the friends that came to the birthday party the excellent and expensive gift you gave him! All the while you are left to smile and grin over something that had no value. You don't want to cause a scene, but you feel shocked that your brother valued you so little while you valued him so much.

Would this hurt you? Would it offend you? I'm sure this is what God feels towards us at times. Our Father gave us the best gift He had which was His Son. (John 3:16) What have we given Him in return?

Since we're discussing the proper way to give love, I would like to share a memory I cherish from my past about my brother's birthday. I might have been eight at the time which means my brother was ten. In preparation for the big day my parents informed me that my brother would be getting a BB gun for his birthday. While I was happy for him, I was also sad because they told me I would not get one. They did not do this out of anger or spite; they did it because it would help me to grow up. Until that time my brother and I had always shared presents, but my parents thought we had reached an age where we both needed to mature. I was ok with it on the outside, but on the inside I was in torment because I really wanted a BB gun.

To make matters worse my parents gave me

the responsibility to present my brother with the ammo for his gun. So I tried to act as if I wasn't hurting when internally I was a basket case. As the evening progressed, I was in turmoil. I wanted a BB gun too, and as the time came to give my brother his presents my dad ducked out the house to get him the gun. When he came back into the house my dad gave my brother the BB gun and he was so ecstatic! I can't remember seeing my brother so happy before, and then all of a sudden it was my turn. Even now, thirty years later, I remember walking up to my brother and with a broken heart I said, *"Neal happy bir…bir…thday."*

Now I wasn't stuttering because my tongue slipped. With tears cascading down my face I was stuttering because I had to give away something that everything within me desired very badly.

As my tears bubbled over, my dad put his arm around me and said *"Let's go outside."* As he escorted me outside I was a mixture of raw emotion. I was thrilled for my brother but heartbroken all at the same time. As we walked down the steps of our patio I looked alongside the wall and saw another brand new BB gun that my parents had bought for me! OMG! I was jumping, hooting, and hollering because of this great and *unexpected* present! In a second my tears of sorrow turned to tears of joy because of how that great gift made me feel. That is the way we should respond to the gifts of God.

Now I can't recall my parents' faces in that moment. I was in shock, and so thankful that little else registered. I remember after grabbing my BB gun I ran and hugged them both with all the strength in my body! Years later God showed me that's how I should show my appreciation for the things He has done for me. I'm sure it made my parents' hearts swell with joy in seeing my face when I received my gift because it makes my heart swell to see my children's faces when they receive theirs. I believe on some level this is how God feels when He sees us enjoying his presents.

My parents gave love by giving me something I desperately desired, and I received their love for me through the gift. However I instantly turned around and returned their love through my hugs, yells, and shouts which they joyously received.

This is the same way it works with God. Giving and receiving love is a two way street. We receive life, purpose, and direction from our God which shows His love for us. Similarly, when we praise Him, He receives our love for Him as we glorify His Name! So let me ask again, "How do you receive Jesus?" *How you give to Christ should be in the same spirit you receive from Him.*

Now this is important! Even though my father

surprised me with this awesome gift, he never asked me for anything *except to obey Him!* See, when you love someone you treat them right and bless them just because you love them. He never said, *"Okay Ray I'm giving you this gift and for it you need to keep your grades up"* or *"you need to wash the dishes."* No! He just gave the gift to me because he is a giver whose happiness is displayed as a result of taking care of his child. My love and submission to his will was all he desired.

Isn't this just like God? He has given you life and manifold blessings and all He expects from you is love and submission to His will for your life. Simply put, He desires two things: For us to love Him with all our heart, mind, and soul, and to follow His teachings.

However, many of us are like the younger brother receiving an awesome birthday gift. We take the gifts of God and we give nothing in return.

Oh we *try* to give *something* to Christ however, what we strive to give is worthless at best. Instead of *staying* in the presence of God and blessing Him for giving us the best He had to offer, we *turn* our backs on God and we run to *everyone else* in the party, excited about the gift God has given us.

From the moment we received His gifts it was no longer about God.

As Christians we love the gifts. In *showing off* our gifts we forget to *worship the giver* of the gift. In church today we shout because we can speak in tongues, we shout because we can sing, and we shout because we have a spirit of prophecy. During the whole time we are reveling in God's gift, we still have our backs turned towards Him.

The sad part of this equation is we think He is pleased with the tackiness of our gift.

If we are really going to *receive* the best from God is it so hard to surmise that we need to reciprocate and *give* our best to God? Haven't we learned yet what we give to God is directly attached to how we receive and perceive God?

Saul received a crown and in return he gave God disobedient attitude. David received a crown and in return he gave God all of his heart. Christ has promised to give each one of us a crown in Glory, but the question is what attitude are you operating in while you wait on God? Have you asked yourself "what are you giving God?"

Our Perception of God

What is your perception of God? To perceive something means immediate or intuitive recognition or appreciation, as of moral, psychological, or aesthetic qualities; intuition; discernment. This is just a fancy way of stating your awareness of God and how you recognize what He does in your life? If you *do not* perceive God or the blessings of God in your life, you won't praise Him for who He is let alone praise Him for what He is doing.

When Christ confronted the Pharisees about their distorted beliefs, He pointed out both of these errors to these spiritually blind men. In John 10:37-38 Christ said, *"If I do not do the works of My Father, do not believe Me; but if I do, though you do not believe Me, believe the works, that you may know and believe that the Father is in Me, and I in Him."*

In essence Christ was letting the Pharisees know these are totally separate issues. As Children of God we are to worship Christ as the Son of God, and we worship Christ for the works and gifts that He has given to us.

This text alone shows that Christ was not seeking credit. He plainly stated to the people, *"if you do not want to believe Me for who I am then believe in Me for the works that I do."* The only way Christ could do the miraculous works He accomplished was if He was sent by God. But the religious elect totally missed His ministry. Since they could not perceive Christ they could not receive Christ.

Here's an example. A man applies for a job online

at a local bank on Tuesday. On Friday morning that company calls him to set up an interview for the following week. After the interview the man gets the job. Do you perceive that God is working?

So let's try another scenario. A Man loses his job on Monday. Tuesday a company calls that he applied to *three years ago* and offers him a job. Do you perceive that God is working? So what is the difference in the two scenarios? In the first scenario it *seemed* like a more natural occurrence. We expect things like this to happen, so we do not perceive that God is working. However in scenario two the *unexpected* happens so we are shocked at how it works out, *thus* we perceive God was working.

Now is God working more in scenario one or two? The answer is God is working in both. The only difference is we *perceive* God is working in scenario two because something happened that we did not expect or foresee.

For many of us our praise and worship of God is based on the *happenings* of life. In both situations God was in control and He performed His perfect will. However, to us we perceive Him doing more for the second man simply because we perceive it to be more *miraculous*.

We should not need to see God to trust that He is moving in our lives.

This shows a stark difference in the maturity of the Christian. If a man lives a life with nothing bad or good happening in his life, does this mean God is not in control over his very existence? Does this mean God has not favored him? Or does a man need to have drama, issues and continuous moral failing's to be considered favored or blessed?

For example, if a church has been in existence for over one hundred years and their membership never grows over twenty members but they can pay their bills and keep the lights on, they are a blessing from God. Likewise, if a church is a tongue-talking, holy ghost filled body of thousands that has been in existence for three years, they are a blessing as well.

Both churches have received gifts from God and both churches are responsible for praising and worshiping God for who He is and what He has done for them. However, many of us will think that the larger church is more *blessed* because it's conception and growth seem more miraculous.

What are we giving back to God? As in the scenario of the brothers, can you imagine God standing in front of you with His mouth open in shock at the gift you repeatedly give Him? *The rule is simple. We should give God what He desires: our hearts and our obedience.*

What's At The Door of Your Heart?

The Bible teaches that two things *wait* outside the door of a man's heart. The first is sin and the second is Christ. This is what the New King James Version says about sin. In Genesis 4:4-6 God told Cain, *"Why are you angry? And why has your countenance fallen? If you do well, will you not be accepted? And if you do not do well, sin lies at the door. And its desire is for you, but you should rule over it."*

However for more clarity I would like to use the King James Version as well. In the King James Version it reads, *"Sin lieth at the door. And unto thee shall be his desire."* Another version says, *"Sin is a crouching beast, striving to get at thee."*

To overcome sin we must understand and guard against it by recognizing the nature of it. First, sin lives outside the door of your heart and wants to make its way inside. Don't allow it because once it enters it will chip away at your spiritual resolve to live holy. Next, sin has desire; it wants your flesh to give it freedom and expression. Lust, greed, envy, jealousy and others are the offspring of sin. Additionally, sin strives, meaning it will always tempt, torment, and tantalize your sinful nature to break its vow with God. Lastly, sin is a beast that cannot be reasoned with or controlled. Simply put, it must be killed.

In the story of Cain and Abel God asked these two brothers to bring an offering to the Lord. The text teaches us that God initiated this by asking them to bring Him a *minchah,* which is a gift. *By requesting a gift, in essence God was asking both men to "show how much they valued Him" and God knew he would see His value through their gift.* Just as the story unfolds we know Cain brought fruit of his land and Abel brought a slaughtered young sheep. When both men presented their offering to God, only Abel's was respected.

When we bring an offering/gift to God, the value of the gift is placed on the giver. When we bring a sacrifice to God, the value of the sacrifice is based on the receiver. So what value do you place on the cross? (1 Corinthians 1:18)

With this in mind we see both men gave of their substance that God had blessed them with. However, both men did not give a gift to God that symbolized the proper relationship that God desired. *See Cain gave a gift, but Abel gave a sacrifice.* When you look at this you see two totally different mindsets towards the one they are giving the substance to.

I am sure that Cain gave a good gift, but his heart was shown to God through what he gave. Abel, on the other hand, gave a great gift showing his heart for God, and this is the reason his offering was accepted.

Family, do not miss this very important point! It was

not the fruit or the sheep that God was looking at. He was looking at the heart. He was looking at the spirit of the giver to see if He would receive the gift or not.

In the time of Cain and Abel, giving of one's "Fruits" were natural occurrences. Travelers were often given fruits and vegetables and gifts as they traveled along their highways. Here in lies the truth of Cain. His view of God was the same as his view of man. There was nothing to separate the two which means he did not hold God in high esteem. *This is the reason his offering wasn't accepted. The gift he gave was a good gift for a man, but it was inappropriate for His God.*

I recently watched a fantastic movie called Anger Management with Jack Nicholson and Adam Sandler. In the movie Jack Nicholson was trying to teach Adam Sandler that there are two types of *anger junkies*, explosive and implosive. With explosive anger a person screams, yells, and mistreats people over the smallest details while the person with the implosive anger takes abuse, criticism and disrespect swallowing it with a grimace until he explodes and lashes out at whoever is around him.

While I loved the definition for both, the movie taught that these types of anger are directed at men. What can you do when they are directed at God?

When we are mad at God we can't take our

anger out on Him, so we take our anger out on others. *This is why we have so many walking wounded in the house of God. We're the only army that willfully kills it soldiers with friendly fire.* This is the same anger that caused Cain to rise up and slay Abel in the middle of the field, and it's the same anger that causes us to kill our brothers' or sisters' spirits in the 21st century.

Because Cain did not receive God correctly, he could not give a correct offering to God which led to his offering being rejected. The Bible then shows the darkness in Cain. He was so wrought with God that his entire disposition, outlook, and frame of mind was changed in an instant. The scripture says, *"And Cain was very angry, and his countenance fell." (Genesis 4:6).*

Saints, when your "countenance" changes, it is so much deeper than your outward expression. Yes, your outward expression changes but so does your inner man. The Bible points out that God spoke directly to Cain regarding this inner darkness.

God said, *"Why are you angry? And why has your countenance fallen?* In this one question we see God trying to reveal a spiritual truth to Cain that many of us miss. Cain knew *exactly* why he was angry. *He just didn't want to admit it.* Cain was angry because he felt cheated by God in His accepting Abel's sacrifice rather than his own.

In this moment of pause in his life, Cain

ultimately made the wrong decision. If he had truthfully assessed his situation, he would have come to God with a repentant heart and asked forgiveness for treating the offering he gave God so casually. Just like my sermon preparation, Cain's gift was not fitting for the King of Glory. All he had to do was submit. But He refused. Instead it became a "me" moment in his life and he sought to feel justified. He became selfish to the point of murdering his brother.

This was his moment of pause. It was a time to seek direction from God. Cain had God's attention. Cain was in God's presence. Cain was in communication with God. All he had to do was look into his heart and let the Lord of Light come in and cast out that inner darkness. However, Cain's refusal to be corrected and ultimately comforted by God shows this had nothing to do with God or Abel. *This was all about Cain; and when we operate in self-denial, we ultimately place ourselves on permanent pause.*

When God confronted Cain He expressly told him that sin *desired* to use him, and we know sin *expressed* itself through Cain and he killed his brother. Cain was not angry at his brother. He was really angry at God. He was angry because he saw his brother favored and he was not.

This is the mindset of many Christians today. Their *service to* God does not line up with their *desires for* God; and when they see someone else get blessed, they become bitter, jealous, and secretly angry at God. Yes, there is always a part of them that is jealous towards their brother or sister, but this is minimal when you consider their mistrust since God did not bless nor favor them.

When we do this we're simply choosing to fail.

Sometimes We Choose To Fail

I remember as a child there were times when I was not as faithful to my classes and studies as I should have been. One time I had failed a test and my teacher informed me I had to get one of my parents to sign it. Hoping to bypass my father I knew instantly this was a job for mom! So I planned to show it to her as soon as we arrived home after school. As I approached my mother I knew I had a fifty-fifty chance of not being disciplined, but I was still nervous. My palms were sweaty, my heart rate was up and when I handed her my paper, she paused.

After a few seconds she led me to the kitchen table where she calmly sat down and asked me why I failed the test? Now saints I believe in the quote, *"To be forewarned is to be forearmed."* Since I knew it was coming I tried to prepare myself for this conversation.

So when she asked me that question I said, *"Mama, the teacher failed me!"*

Being in the fifth grade I figured open denial was the best option. Men of God have been doing this for years. Adam did it in the garden when he blamed Eve. Cain did it when God asked where his brother was and I was doing it now. The only thing that saved me that day was accepting my mistakes as my own.

She slowly shook her head and she said, *"Ray, how can the teacher fail you?"* Being ten I wasn't prepared for this question, so I merely shrugged. After a short pause she asked me, *"Did the teacher take the test?"* I said, *"No"* with an immediate sinking feeling in the pit of my stomach. *"Did you have help on the test?"* I said, *"No."* *"Did anyone else write on your test?"* With a long sigh, I replied, *"No."* Her final question put the nail in my coffin. *"So who failed you?"* My answer, *"I did."*

My mother went on to say that she was glad for me taking responsibility for my actions, but I was still disciplined. She said the punishment would have been worse the longer I tried to deny my responsibilities to my teacher, my parents, and more importantly myself.

When God reasons with us it is to get us to do the same thing. *We must accept responsibility for our actions and our inactions.* We must accept that we are not giving our best to God in this test of life. He knows we are failing the test and more importantly we know we are failing the test, but instead of being responsible we try to slide by on the grace of God.

Life can beat you down. Family members can get on your last nerve, but every day we live we have a choice to make. We have sin that lies at our door and we have Christ at our door. We are all given the opportunity to allow only one to come in per day. Which one will you allow to come in? *Will you open your heart to Sin or to God? Only one can come in. So, "choose you this day who you will serve." I've made my choice. What is yours?*

Who's That Knocking? Should I Let Them In?

A few years ago I remember listening to a standup comedian tell a joke about the necessity of being ready to meet the coming of Christ. The punch line of his joke showed that some people would be in adulterous affairs, some would be liars, others slanderers but many would not be ready for the moment that Christ arrived. This joke to me, while funny, was also very sad because it showed the refusal of man to accept the free gift that he was being offered.

In the joke the announcement of Christ's arrival began with a simple gesture of a knock on the door. After hearing the knock the various people in the joke stopped momentarily to find out who was knocking on the door. In essence they had a moment of "pause" before they went to see who was standing at the door. This is done so they are able to determine if they want to stop their activity or continue by dismissing the person at the door.

When they asked, "*Who is it?*" and a voice replied, "*Jesus,*" they immediately sprang into action because they all wanted to be presentable to God before He saw them. *However this is the wrong attitude to have with God.*

Isaiah said in Chapter 64:6, *"But we are all like an unclean thing, and all our righteousnesses are like filthy rags; we all fade as a leaf, and our iniquities, like the wind, Have taken us away."* If you know you are as filthy rags, why are you trying to hide yourselves from God? He already knows! So instead of you trying to hide your sins from God, like Adam and Eve in the garden and the people in this joke, just be thankful that God came and knocked on the door!

In Revelation 3: 20 Christ said, *"Behold, I stand at the door and knock. If anyone hears My voice and opens the door, I will come in to him and dine with him, and he with*

Me." This text implies that the doorway of a man's heart is *naturally* closed to Christ.

However, it can be opened in Jesus Name! Even though the way is shut initially, God still makes His presence known and He's available to us by knocking on the door of our hearts.

Imagine going to visit your neighbor across the street to check on their welfare. Before you enter their home you knock to let them know you are outside. This is an instinctual trait that we all have. We have been taught from childhood to knock before entering. The knocking by Christ shows us several things about our God.

First, He wants to alert us to His presence. Secondly, knocking announces to individuals that Christ is seeking entrance to our hearts and admittance into our lives. It also teaches us Christ's admittance is a personal choice where we have to do our part and let Him come in. Finally, and this is truly a scary situation, if Christ is not allowed into the home, He leaves.

Yes To Savior, No To Lord

As I have looked back on my life, I have learned that most of my pauses have nothing to do with

Christ being my Savior, but it has everything to do with him being my Lord. See we all want salvation because none of us want to die and go to hell. That is the easy part.

However, since many of us refuse to kill our flesh, it causes our natural disobedient nature to rise up in our lives. When this happens we rebel against Christ and His teaching. Then to get us back on the right path God has to send us into a season of pause.

Many people want to receive the Savior aspect of Christ, but they seldom desire to submit to His Lordship.

We live in a time where many people *"say"* they love God, but they really do not *"know"* the God they *"say"* they love. We see this every day in our society where Christians desire the *excess* of God instead of living a *submitted* life to God.

People crave the security of salvation plus the freedom to live and do whatever they desire. Quite the contrary, this is not the teachings of Christ. Our God called us to die to self, not thrive to self.

If we turn our eyes to Apostle Paul, only a few weeks from being crucified he wrote to Timothy these words found in II Timothy 4: 3-5, *"For the time will come when they will not endure sound doctrine, but according to their own desires, because they have itching ears, they will heap up for themselves teachers; and they will turn their ears away from the truth, and be turned aside to fables. But you be watchful in all things, endure afflictions, do the work of an evangelist, fulfill your ministry."*

These words echo our generation. We live in a time when people desire to live a spiritual life; however, many balk when it comes to the boundaries that Christ has commanded. So instead of submitting to God in the trouble areas of their lives, many seek for new revelations or theories so they may pattern themselves after their hearts' desires all the while denouncing the true doctrine of Jesus Christ. This group of people seeks leaders to tickle their ears as they pacify their flesh which will ultimately turn them from the truth of God

However, notice Paul followed this summation by telling Timothy that it does not matter what everyone else does, his job was to endure! Paul's saying, *"But You"* means the entire direction of his teaching has changed. This is Paul's way of sharing with Timothy that he was not supposed to live like this!

So as we come to a close in Chapter 2, please let me earnestly say if you are angry with God because you feel life is passing you by, please pray before continuing this book. We must regain our focus on God because the only way we can move forward is to have the right relationship with Him and patiently wait to be pulled out of our spiritual mud-hole. I know it might not feel good, but this is where many of us must resolve to be like Job. We must understand that we all have got to wait until our change comes.

Study Guide

Chapter 2: What Are You Waiting For?

1. Are you waiting on God or is God waiting on you? Since you have read this book have you seen any areas of pause in your life where God withdrew His presence or anointing from your life? Can you share of your experiences?

2. As a child who has been given the ultimate gift, what do you think is appropriate to give back to God? Is there anything less than your total mind, body, and soul that you think would be worthy enough to give to God?

3. Think of how you received your favorite present? Was the giving of the gift a surprise to you? Since you know tomorrow isn't promised, is it possible that you can see your new tomorrow as a present?

4. Why are you on pause? Have you chosen to fail? Is there an area of your life you know God desires more from you but you are rebelling against His will? As you patiently wait on God what do you think He's trying to teach you in this season of

pause? What character flaws do you notice when you begin to enter these seasons?

5. Identify as many reasons as you can as to why God can't use you for His purpose. Then compare your excuses to the awesomeness of God. Do you believe God made a mistake when He called you to Himself? Read Romans 8:37. How does this scripture compare to your reasons?

CHAPTER 3

Enlighted, But Still In The Dark

And behold, there came a man named Jairus, and he was a ruler of the synagogue. And he fell down at Jesus' feet and begged Him to come to his house.
~Luke 8:41

Out of difficulties grow miracles.
~Jean De La Bruyere

Why did you come to Christ? Why did you submit your life to God? For many of us we came to Christ for a reason, for a purpose. When I met the Lord at Greater Zion MBC I was stuck on pause. At the time I was in a very dark place and no one could help me out of the predicament I had placed myself in.

So when I came to Christ, I did not come out of love or

sweet fellowship. I came to Him out of necessity because I was in the worst pain in my young life, and I had nowhere else to turn.

I was separated from my family, distant from my brother, and I had no friends that wanted to be around me. To make matters worse, it was my 25th birthday and I had no one to share it with.

Does this sound like a blessing waiting to happen? Does it sound like a blessed place to be? Yes it was! Remember all coins are positive. Perceived negatives in the physical will always be a blessing in the spiritual, if you look through the right lens.

This was a blessed place because I had nowhere to turn to but God. Being that I was ostracized from my friends and family, I decided to go to church. I did not go because I was looking for a radical worship experience. I went because being in a room full of strangers felt better to me than being in my dorm room all day by myself.

At that time I was at the lowest of my lows. I had lost my apartment because I wasn't faithful in paying my rent. I had recently blown up my car because I wasn't seeing to its necessary maintenance. I was on the verge of losing my job because of my bad attitude and poor work ethic.

So things weren't on the up and up in my life.

Being that I was employed but had nowhere to

stay, I began living in a refurbished prison dorm for employees that worked for the Texas Department of Criminal Justice. As you might have guessed these dorms are nowhere like the Omni hotel. The rooms were about 10 by 10 that contained two twin beds and a very small linen closet. There was one bathroom that four suite mates had to share. Between the constant fights among the people in the dorms and a roommate who would drink himself into a stupor then pass out in his own vomit three nights a week, I felt like I was literally in my own prison.

The truly sad part of this story is I had no idea how to get off pause. There's nothing worse than being in a situation and you have no idea how to get yourself out of it. So I did the only thing I could do. I picked up a Bible and I started to read.

However, things didn't immediately change. I started reading the Bible every night and it gave me some internal relief, but my external world was still in chaos. *Keep in mind Jesus will always calm your internal storm before He calms your external storm. This way you know Jesus has all power in His hands.*

When I came to Greater Zion that morning, I purposed to sit at the back of church. Like many people who come to church, I wanted to be in the house of God but not too close to the power of God. At that time it was just something about sitting close to the pulpit that was very eerie to me. I felt like I just couldn't trust that the power of God would not reach out in a lightning bolt and strike me down while burning me to a cinder!

After doing a quick scan of the people surrounding me, I didn't see anyone I knew so I began to relax. Half way through the service Pastor Michael C. Davis stood up and he asked for anyone that needed prayer to come to the altar. However, being stubborn and prideful I stayed right where I was. I knew I *needed* to go to the altar, but I was not about to *show* people I needed prayer! To me people that went to the altar were weak, and even in my foolishness I dug in my heels because of my pride and ignorance.

Do you know I was right? Weak people do go to the altar for prayer so that God can make them strong!

After a few seconds of soft worship music I began to hear Pastor Davis's voice open the door to my spirit as he began to pray. He simply said, "*Just let it go*" and "BAM!" just like in the old Batman comics where the words popped onto the TV screen showing extra emphasis, my spirit was bombarded as the Holy Spirit rushed into me. It felt like a deafening explosion had just been triggered in my body.

That momentary experience is something I will never

forget. *I immediately started reaching for more and more of that presence because I knew it was too good not to be God.*

When the Spirit landed on me the tears started flowing, snot started flying, and I was caught up in The Spirit! I can't tell you how the prayer ended, I can't tell you what he preached about that day, and I can't tell you who saw me sitting on that pew crying like a little baby, but I *can* say God had taken control.

For the remainder of the service God had pressed "pause" on my life and it was the sweetest fellowship I had ever known.

After church I vaguely remember the drive home. However, I do remember my spirit was dancing inside my body feeling like it was hopping on pins and needles. I was exuberant and excited all at the same time. In some ways this was my spiritual birthing. Since my spirit had been asleep to Christ, it would be natural to feel this way. In some ways it was like a powerful engine, which had just been turned on for the first time, and it vibrated with Holy Ghost power.

Upon coming back to my dorm room, that no longer felt like a prison cell, I just wanted to call someone and share this great news, so I started dialing everyone I knew. But sadly, no one answered the phone. I called family, friends, cousins, neighbors, old girlfriends and folks that I thought hated me, but no one greeted me with a hearty, "H*ello*!"

I did not know it then, but God wanted "my" time and He would not share me with anyone else.

Finally, I began to get discouraged and I decided to watch a Christian video I had borrowed from the unit chaplain. The sermon was entitled, *"Man-Child in the Promised Land"* by Bishop T.D. Jakes. As soon as I began to watch the tape "BAM!" Batman Time Again! I got hit by the Spirit of God again, but this time it was different. This time I wasn't just caught up in God. This time when the Spirit hit me I was out like a light!

When I came too, I slowly began pulling myself off the floor and I noticed two things. One, the service was ending on the tape and two, I was speaking in tongues. At that time I had no idea what this strange language was, but I knew spiritually this *had to be* God moving in my life.

I wanted to share this particular story of my life because I wanted you to know that when I came to God I came because pain was my guide. For many of us pain is always our guide when we begin to seek earnestly for Jesus. Pain is what brought me to Christ and pain is what brought Jairus to Christ.

When you read the story of Jairus, you see he is a man that's truly stuck on pause. Although he is seen only once in the gospels, his short walk with Christ is full of Theological and Christological revelation. From the outset of his story we see two things that stand out about him. First, he's a man with great authority within the local church. Second, his daughter is at the point of death and there's nothing he can do about it.

When we see Jairus we must understand the complex situation he is in. Jairus is a man who is caught up in emotional and spiritual turmoil. Jairus is a synagogue official and his name means *enlightened,* but from his reactions to Christ we see there isn't any light in him. The word enlightened defined means to be well informed: having a sound and open-minded understanding of all the facts. It also means free of ignorance, prejudice, or superstition.

Just because a person has a title in the church does not mean he knows the God of the church.

So is Jairus enlightened? He is enlightened to the Law of God; however, he is completely in the dark when it comes to the Grace of God through Christ Jesus. We get a glimpse of his character when we look at his reaction to Christ's first sermon in Luke 4.

For Christ's initial sermon, He preached Isaiah 61:1-3 which says, *"The Spirit of the LORD is upon Me, Because He has anointed Me To preach the gospel to the poor; He has sent Me to heal the brokenhearted, To proclaim liberty to the captives And recovery of sight to the blind, To set at liberty those who are oppressed; To proclaim the acceptable year of the LORD."*

By Christ's statement we can derive that He was speaking by Divine Appointment, He was anointed and set apart for a particular work, and He was to communicate the "Good News" to those who were sick of sin, poor in spirit, and discouraged with this life. Upon this announcement Christ said, *"Today this Scripture is fulfilled in your hearing."*

Many of us today when witnessing a young preacher give his first sermon grant them a lot of latitude in delivering the Word. We understand the fear that comes with standing in the pulpit and speaking God's Word before our family, our friends, and the very people we use to do all manners of evil things with, as well as standing before a Holy God. With that knowledge in mind we know they are shaking in their boots, but as long as they stick to the Word of God we always give them encouragement and accolades.

In my time as a pastor and minister I have seen all types of "introductory" sermons. I've seen preachers barely able to stand for fright. I've seen some preachers preach longer than movies. Then there are those who teach, those who preach, and those who whoop and holler so loud you have no idea what they were saying. However, one thing remained constant. *They were given time to say whatever God instructed them to say.*

However, this was Christ. He did not come for titles or accolades. He came to save mankind from their sins. So He began addressing their need for a savior by sharing a Word that would require the people to focus on their sin rather that critiquing His sermon and pulpit protocol.

In almost twenty years of preaching I have learned if a preacher or pastor ever wanted to make people upset from the pulpit, all he had to do was show them who they really are. If you ever want to silence a church and never be invited back to preach, show the people themselves. How is this accomplished? *Preach on the sins of the people.*

As a pastor I have learned that sermons that are designed to address a person's salvation are greatly received, as well as sermons that cover coming blessings, or the beauty of heaven, or even maturity in Christ. However, when I preach over sin, you can hear a pin drop in the sanctuary. *The reason for this is people hate to be exposed.*

Preachers, if you want God to say, "well done my good and faithful servant" you must preach celebratory messages as well as convicting messages. We are called to preach the truth of the gospel not just the feel-good aspects of the gospel.

Christ spoke of two instances of the Jews

history when God chose to send His blessing outside of the commonwealth of Israel. He said, *"You know what? When God shut up heaven for forty-two months He didn't send Elijah to the Jews after the brook of Kidron dried up. He sent him to this little old heathen widow woman in Zarephath."*

Now if you know your Bible and you know your history, the last people the Jews wanted to be recognized were people from Zarephath. More importantly, He sent him to a widow woman. He was a prophet. Because of their religious belief system, they knew a prophet had no business being around an unmarried woman.

Think about it. In today's society, how would it look for a single preacher to spend his days and nights away with an unmarried woman living close to the red-light district? How many of you cringe when you hear the words "Gürrllll!!! Do you know what Pastor did??? I heard he was seen with that trifling, unmarried, ex-stripper who lives down by the tracks!"

As you know in many churches today the members would have been ready to vote him out and elect a new pastor the next week! However the text never says there was anything illicit about God sending Elijah to Zarapeth. There was nothing recorded that pointed to some type of affair. The Jews simply did not like this because God sent a prophet to bless someone they disliked.

Do you think they were mad at God? Do you think their countenance changed like Cain's? I mean He is the one who sent Elijah to Zarapeth. Since they couldn't fight God they decided to take their frustration out on the man who shared the word with them, Christ?

In His second reference Christ spoke of the healing of the Syrian Naaman. That's when the people of God lost it! Forgive me for adding hilarity in this book, but in addressing this scene in my mind, I compare the response of the people in the sanctuary to the people in the movie Airplane! In the scene everyone in the cabin of the plane is calm and peaceful; however, as soon as the stewardess comes across the microphone and says, *"I'm sorry but we're out of coffee,"* the people go crazy! A riot ensued! People began fighting, some were crying, others praying. It was utter chaos!

Getting back to this scene, let me say when you show people their true selves expect the worst to come out in them.

It's so sad to read how *fast* the people, who began *praising* Christ during the first portion of His sermon, ended up trying to *kill Him* in the conclusion because of His message of conviction. Now none of these people were alive when these two judgments of God happened. However, their pride caused them to sin just like Cain, and their sin wanted to work through them in killing the Christ!

Preachers, if you preach a word of conviction, expect some folks to be ready to try to kill you too, and they will do this by attacking your character.

Luke 4:28-30 says, *"So all those in the synagogue, when they heard these things, were filled with wrath, and rose up and thrust Him out of the city; and they led Him to the brow of the hill on which their city was built, that they might throw Him down over the cliff. Then passing through the midst of them, He went His way."*

So here comes Jairus to Christ. Here is a man who once tried to be a party in killing Christ; now he's a man who ends up worshipping Christ because he's in need of Christ. *No, he doesn't fully understand Christ, but none of us do when we first meet Him.* Ironically, many of us despise Christ until we get stuck on pause. He came to Christ out of his pain, but now he has to fall on his knees to worship Him.

Just A Face In The Crowd

Some might look at Jairus as a big man in the church. However, with a problem like this he's simply another face in the crowd anxiously waiting on the Master to arrive. He knows Christ is the only one who can do what he desires to be done. He knows Christ is the only one with "saving grace."

So understand, Jairus is not coming to God because of who He is; he is coming to God because he has a problem he can't solve. In the temple Jairus might have been a ruler and he might know where everything belongs, but when it came to his daughter's healing he was left dumbfounded and powerless.

How could he cure his daughter? How could he stop her from dying? He knew he did not have the power or authority over life and death but he knew of one who did! Jesus Christ. So he put his pretenses and his spiritual superiority aside and he humbled himself by stripping himself of his title, his beliefs, and his church expectations. Once he accomplished this he simply became a worried father in need of divine healing for someone he loved dearly.

No matter who you are, sooner or later, in life you will need the grace of God. There are plenty of people who claim Christ doesn't exist. However, when death is close they run to Christ as quickly as they can. Jairus did not accept the message of Christ, but His love for his daughter brought him to the Master nevertheless. So who cares how you came to Christ! I just praise God that you came!

If our lives were like ice cream and peach cobbler all the time, there would be no need for Jesus. However, the imminent death of his daughter had brought Jairus to his knees. As a man with position in the church he would *turn away* from Christ, but as a father who loves his daughter it made him *turn to Christ. When the problems of life come, we should be thankful because it serves as a constant reminder that we don't have it all together and God is the only true source of power we have.*

So while we may criticize and point our finger at Jairus, we can't condemn him. We really can't be mad at Jairus because most of us are exactly like him. I know I was.

If you are like me you shunned Christ when you could handle all of your problems. Before you had a need you couldn't meet or a disease you couldn't control were you concerned about God? Were you worried about your soul's salvation before you were stuck on pause in an area of your life? The scripture says, *"And he fell down at Jesus' feet and begged Him to come to his house, for he had an only daughter about twelve years of age, and she was dying. But as He went, the multitudes thronged Him."*

When you have a problem that's outside of something you can't fix, you're going to be quick to come to Christ. Please notice I did not say the church. I said Christ.

Many people believe their strength is in the church building. Some believe their strength is in the pastor they follow. However, this isn't true in the least. Buildings can be destroyed and men of God will fall into sin. Both of these are simply masks that God will remove from your life so that you understand He alone is the only one you can count on. When you have a real problem you don't have to wait until you get to church, nor do you have to wait to talk to your pastor. When you are in a bad place in life and you have real problems on your hands, you can come to the altar, in your spirit, anywhere and at any time.

At least Jairus got it right. When in doubt or trouble run to Jesus!

Dealing with death is never a fun experience. When death invades our ranks, even the staunchest religious activist pauses and become quiet in retrospect. As scripture teaches death is the last enemy we must overcome. (1st Corinthians 15:26) Death is something that we must trust God to take us through to see life on the other side. Death will make the staunchest sinner into the most seasoned saint. We can debate about communion, and if the body of Christ needs to be a cracker or wafer, but when it comes to death, things get real serious real fast.

When Jairus came to Christ he was broken and contrite. All of the glamour and show was gone. He was a man that was held together by one single thought. He thinks, *"If Jesus can heal others, then maybe He can heal my daughter?"*

An Audience With The Master

The issue of getting to Jesus has nothing to do with, "can Jesus heal my daughter?" We know He can. Philippians 3:20 assures of this fact. The text says, *"Now to Him who is able to do exceedingly abundantly above all that we ask or think, according to the power that works in us."*

We know God has the power to heal. But the question is do you have enough patience to wait for your opportunity? Remember James 5: 11, "Indeed we count them blessed who endure."

Notice in his conversation there was no theological debate. There was no reminder of who he was, his position in the church, or how much tithes his family had paid over the years. This was serious and Jairus needed help that only God could give. In his eyes he only saw that his daughter was dying and his time was running out.

Keep in mind it's during the rough times that God plants, grows, and matures our faith. Luke 18:1 says, "And He spoke a parable unto this end: That men should always pray and not faint." When we are in the process of enduring for Christ, fainting is not an option.

If Christ did not faint for us while enduring the full weight of God's wrath on the Cross, then fainting is not an option for us. We must endure. If you ask me how long it will take, how long you will have to wait for your audience with the Master, I would say that depends on how badly you want to be in His presence.

Do you have the faith to try to press through the crowds like Zacchaeus? Here was a little man who had great faith when he heard Jesus was coming to town. Once he heard Christ had arrived he tried to see Him, but he couldn't fight through the pressure of the crowds because he lacked the physical strength. Did he give up? No, He would not be defeated so he found another way to enter the Masters presence! Luke 19:1-5 says, *"Then Jesus entered and passed through Jericho. Now behold, there was a man named Zacchaeus who was a chief tax collector, and he was rich. And he sought to see who Jesus was, but could not because of the crowd, for he was of short stature. So he ran ahead and climbed up into a sycamore tree to see Him, for He was going to pass that way."*

Zacchaeus did not allow his financial position, lack of strength, or his lack of height to stop him from entering the presence of Christ. Sure, sometimes it's hard to enter into prayer because of worry, doubt, and frustration. All of these are things that stop us from entering the spirit realm through prayer. However, just because it doesn't work once does that mean you stop your pursuit of Christ and your answer from God?

Zacchaeus tried to get an audience with Christ like everyone else. He tried to enter through the crowd, but he just couldn't do it. *In spite of all this his determination did not diminish; it only grew.* So he did the unexpected. He found where Christ was going and he put himself ahead of Jesus, just so he could see him.

If you know the direction in which Christ is going, then you have a roadmap to find Him. The map to Christ is the attributes of God. We pursue Him based on His teachings and His ways. When we follow them in obedience, it will eventually lead us to Him.

This was a man that was not merely curious about Christ but one that *had to* enter into his presence. This was a man that desired an audience with the Master. To gain entrance he had to seek Him with a whole heart.

You have to be focused in your pursuit of Christ and you have to keep coming to Him, even when you don't feel like it. I am sure Jairus did not *feel* like being in the presence of Christ. His personal and spiritual convictions would have set him apart from the others who came to see Jesus.

Many who came to Christ were the diseased and infirmed. However in Jairus you have a leader of the synagogue who has the same basic needs as everyone else. He needed God to do something for him that he could not do for himself. So he stood on the banks of the sea because his need for his daughter's healing outweighed his disbelief that Jesus was not this Christ.

When we get to the place where we have a "whatever it takes attitude" towards getting in the presence of God, we will find ourselves blessed because we are moving in a deeper more intimate realm of faith. First let's look at little faith to see how we matriculate from level to level in faith.

The Problem With Little Faith

And he fell down at Jesus' feet and begged Him to come to his house.

There is a problem with little faith. In our Bible Christ referred to three types of faith: little faith, faith, and great faith. During his time of walking the earth he encountered the first two forms of faith most often with people having roots in the religious community.

When it came to the Apostles during the three and a half years Christ walked this earth with them, He constantly informed them they were operating in little faith. In Matthew 8:23-27 the text says, *"Now when He got into a boat, His disciples followed Him. And suddenly a great tempest arose on the sea, so that the boat was covered with the waves. But He was asleep. Then His disciples came to Him and awoke Him, saying, and "Lord,* save us"! We are perishing!" But He said to them, "Why are you fearful, O you of little faith?" Then He arose and rebuked the winds and the sea, and there was a great calm. So the men marveled, saying, "Who can this be, that even the winds and the sea obey Him?"

It is one of the most preached New Testament scriptures that teaches us we are all works in progress. Many men and women of God point to the statement of Christ *before* they entered troubled waters that they would inevitably make it to the other side. However, what happens to the person that missed that speech? What happens to the person that was not paying attention?

The singular truth of this text is simple and easy to understand. Is Christ on the boat? Yes? Then you're safe. It does not matter what direction you are going in as long as you have Christ on the Ship!

When the disciples awoke Christ, their fear and panic was evident. Seeing these men as the twelve Apostles is almost laughable. They were on a ship with the Master of the Universe and they were in fear for their lives. Upon waking Christ condemns their faith and said, *"Why are you fearful, O you of little faith?"*

With Jesus there is no need to worry, fret, or be fearful of the outcome because Christ is our protection during the storms of life. With Him we are totally secure; however,

Christ was seeking to teach them to take a moment to look "within" and assess their own faith.

When we look at the disciples, although we see them at their lowest, I give God praise for this view of the disciples. I praise Him because this lets me know that nobody gets it right the first time, or the second, or the third. It takes time for your faith to grow.

You can tell anybody that will listen that you have faith. However you will never know the kind of faith you possess until you are tested by the storms of life. Remember faith is birthed, developed, and matured in the storm.

If you ask how Jairus could have little faith, it is seen in his approach to Christ. He entreated Christ to come to his house to lay his hands on his daughter. His faith was limited because he was looking through the wrong lens.

Jairus saw Christ in a limited role which limited his faith. Even though Christ knew Jairus had the wrong perception of who He was, He still allowed Jairus to lead… for a little while.

He says, "*Christ, I need You to come to my house. I need You to lay Your hands on my daughter. She's sick, Jesus. You know she's about to get to the point of dying.*" And here comes Christ; He says, "*All right. I'm going to follow you to your house.*"

I thank God that Christ was willing to come to

Jairus's house. It is a blessing to know we serve a God that will take care of His children and bless them according to their faith. However notice Jairus wanted to *supervise* His blessing from God.

Jairus wanted God to follow three main steps. First, he wanted Christ to walk with him to his house. Second, he asked Christ to Lay Hands on His daughter. Third, *only then* could he spiritually see her being healed.

Do you see the problem with Jairus? Do you see his little faith? Do you see how he tried to *limit* Christ? In the mind of Jairus if God does not follow his prayer specifically to the "T" then it wouldn't work.

Many of us choose this pathway when we are in prayer.

Instead of asking God to work out His will in our lives according to His design, we try to oversee the blessings of God. It's not that we don't want to be blessed, but we want God to bless us in the way we want to be blessed. This limits our faith and it hinders our process.

The Blessing Of Great Faith

In Matthew 8:5-13 Christ meets a centurion whose faith shocks Him. Notice both Jairus and the Centurion were asking for healing for someone close to themselves. Jairus was asking for his daughter while the Centurion was asking for his servant.

Both men came to the Master and both men entreated Christ to heal on their behalf. However while Jairus tried to control his blessing by having Christ follow Him to his house, the Centurion gave Christ free reign to bless him by saying there was no need for Christ to come under his roof. This is the foundational difference between little faith versus great faith. *It's your perception of God and what He can do in your life.*

In the mind of Jairus he viewed Christ as a human with God-like power. However, the centurion viewed Christ as God in human form.

We see this in their treatment of Christ. We see that Jairus opened his home to Christ *only to receive healing for his daughter.* If his daughter had not been sick, Christ would have *never* been *invited* into Jairus' house.

Knowing this we must be thankful for the sickness of Jairus's daughter. Her illness accomplished three things. It allowed her father to establish a relationship with Christ. Her illness brought the presence of God into her home, and God performed a miracle in the house by restoring her back to life.

In the eyesight of the Centurion he viewed himself unworthy for Christ to come into his house.

In Matthew 8: 8 he said, *"Lord, I am not worthy that You should come under my roof. But only speak a word, and my servant will be healed."*

Even though both men had status in the secular world, only one was truly humble in the spiritual world. Jairus was a Jew, one of the chosen people; yet he did not recognize Christ for who He was. On the other hand the Centurion was a gentile, one of the discounted and lost souls who were disconnected from Israel, yet he knew exactly who he was dealing with.

His denial to Christ was not because he did not want Christ to enter his home. He simply felt unworthy knowing he was talking to God. This is how we should all entreat Christ, with true humbleness and a lowly spirit. This text shows the conviction of the centurion because all men are truly unworthy to be in the presence of God.

When we see Jairus and his small faith in operation, we see for him to believe in God he wanted Christ to jump through certain hoops. However the Centurion didn't need any of this. He simply wanted Christ to speak a Word (of healing) and he knew his servant would be healed.

This is one of the main differences between little faith and big faith. Little faith wants to see "how" the healing is done. Great Faith does not care "how" it's done just as long as it is done.

This is why he did not get frustrated or flustered around Christ's ability to heal his servant. He did not view Christ's healing ability as *faith*. He viewed it as *fact*. He knew Christ could heal, deliver, and set free at one Word.

Notice at the beginning of the text Christ was set to go with the Centurion. *"And Jesus said to him, 'I will come and heal him.'"* However the centurion stopped Christ and said, "Speak a Word (of healing)." Christ was going to do the very thing for the centurion that he did for Jairus, but the responsibility for *recognizing* Christ fell to the centurion.

If Christ really is God then why did He need to come to the centurion's house? If God really is God why does He need to bless us the exact way we want Him to bless us? Wouldn't it be better if we all operated in Great Faith and said, "God, just speak a Word!"

For this statement of faith in Christ, our Lord and Savior marveled at this man's faith. He might have been unworthy in his own eyes, but he was truly worthy in God's eyes because he had the confidence that Christ could and would do whatever He said because of who He is.

Then Christ issues one of the greatest but also one of the saddest comments in this text. He said, *"Assuredly, I say to you, I have not found such great faith, not even in Israel!"*

When Christ made this statement, He was not talking to the Centurion but to the men and women of Israel that were following Him. In making this statement we see a glorious revelation of Christ. *Every child of God should have this type of faith.*

Jesus was telling his followers that this is how you should believe in me!

The last time I checked, Buddha and Mohammed were still in the grave. It grieves my heart to see their servants are more faithful in their pursuit of a false god than we are in our service to the True and Living God. As a final word of prophecy Christ said, *"And I say to you that many will come from east and west, and sit down with Abraham, Isaac, and Jacob in the kingdom of Heaven. But the sons of the kingdom will be cast out into outer darkness. There will be weeping and gnashing of teeth."*

As Christ saw through the faith of the Centurion, He spoke a word about the future of the Kingdom of God. He said that many will come from various places outside the commonwealth of Israel to sit down at the wedding feast of the Lamb and the Church. The entire globe will be searched and many will come from various beliefs and faiths to trust in the One True God. However, because of their pride and arrogance, many of the *"original* chosen people" will be discarded.

The Old Testament Jews were the original chosen people. However, from the inception of the New Testament and the acceptance of the gentiles into the family of God we are now the "chosen" people. Will we morph into their religious superiority? Or will we continue in faith while trusting and believing in the Most High?

For those who do not make it to the wedding feast to be among these great men their end is dreadful and unimaginable. They will be tormented and grief stricken.

As a former Prison Chaplain, one of the worst parts of my job was giving an offender a death notice. When they came into my office most were already nervous and upset because they knew a call to the chaplain's office, nine times out of ten, was not good. Some even began crying before they even came into my office. However, in the end when I told them the bad news, it hit all of them the same way. They were damaged and hurt, but their secondary emotion was disgust.

They were disgusted because of being locked up behind bars away from their family during this rough time. The real weight hits them with the realization that they are in prison because of the bad choices they made while living on the outside.

The worst moments came when they realized

they *chose to put themselves in that position by choosing to break the law. That was the hardest part for many of them.* It was not the death of the loved one. They understood that death was a part of life. However the real pain they felt, was knowing that they were separated from their family in the time of mourning because of their choices.

This is what outer darkness is. It is a place where *we choose to go* because we make choices that are not in His will. How long will Christ have to stand with outstretched arms before we realize everything we are and hope to become is found in Him? How long will we need scriptures like Proverbs 1:20-25 which says, *"Wisdom calls aloud outside; She raises her voice in the open squares. She cries out in the chief concourses, At the openings of the gates in the city She speaks her words: "How long, you simple ones, will you love simplicity? For scorners delight in their scorning, And fools hate knowledge. Turn at my rebuke; Surely I will pour out my spirit on you; I will make my words known to you. Because I have called and you refused I have stretched out my hand and no one regarded, Because you disdained all my counsel, And would have none of my rebuke."*

For those that fail to heed the warnings of Christ there is weeping and gnashing of teeth. It is being separated from those you love because you chose to follow your flesh and not your spirit.

If you are a person who feels you have missed God in some fundamental way, I surmise you might feel like this, weeping and gnashing of teeth. If you are not demonstrating great faith don't be surprised when you lose the Masters attention for a moment. However, one of the fastest ways for a person to learn to move in faith is for them to be stuck on pause.

This happened to Jairus when a little old lady walked up and touched the hem of His garment.

Study Guide

Chapter 3: Enlighted, But Still In The Dark

1. Describe a time in your life when you were enlightened by God with a revelation tailor made for your current situation? When He delivered you, healed you, or spoke to you how did you respond to the blessing of God?

2. Look back at your life before you came to the knowledge of Jesus Christ. How did you feel about Christians them? How did you respond to those that spoke to you about Jesus? Between that time and now have you ran into or met any of the people God used to share the gospel with you? If you haven't seen any of them what do you think they will say about you now?

3. When the word of God goes forward in the church what "type" of word leads to a more enlightened walk with Christ? Is a word of salvation? Repentance? Conviction? Or prosperity? Which one makes you shout more and which one makes you look you're your heart?

4. If you could have an audience with the Master what would you say to Him? What would you ask Him? Would you come with a spirit of humility or with a spirit of entitlement?

5. Tell of a time where you operated in little faith? Tell of a time where you operated in great faith? Now speak of the things that you had to endure or lessons you learned from Christ during that maturation process? What caused you to stand firm on God's word when you previously were shaking in your boots?

CHAPTER 4

Uh, Jesus? – I'm Stuck!

For he had an only daughter about twelve years of age, and she was dying. But as He went, the multitudes thronged Him.
~Luke 8:42

There are no mistakes in life, only lessons.
~Anonymous

Jairus had just accomplished his goal! For all his issues, inadequacies, and his little faith he had reached the Master, entreated Him, and Jesus had agreed to come into his home to heal his sick child. *Isn't that just like Christ?* Even though Jairus saw Christ in a limited capacity, our Master was still willing to work within that small scope to bring Jairus to the full realization to who He really was. (Ephesians 1:17)

Nevertheless we can't be too hard on Jairus. Every strong saint of God begins their walk towards maturity as a babe in Christ wobbling on weak legs of faith. Therefore, this is good news! God doesn't despise small beginnings (Job 8:7) and neither should we!

As they left the shore Jairus took it upon himself to *lead* Jesus to his home which begs the question, *"Do you think Jesus knew where Jairus lived?"* I'm sure He did. Jesus was Omnipresent, meaning He was capable of being wherever He needed to be. One second He was on a mountain and the next He was walking on a raging sea. He was Omnipotent, meaning He had all power in His hands. He had the power to heal the lame, cure the sick, and raise the dead. He also was Omniscient, meaning He knew all things. This is why the religious leaders of His day could never confuse, trick, or deceive Him.

So why did Jesus allow Jairus to take the lead? Because trusting God is a daily process which requires a person to take incremental steps of faith as we decrease so Christ can increase in our lives. *No one instantly trusts God with all their life decisions.* This is accomplished through our daily struggles as we learn to depend more and more upon the personhood of Jesus Christ.

Here's a good introductory question for the next section. *Have you ever met someone famous? Like a professional football player, or maybe a singer? How about the President? What did it feel like to be in that person's presence? Were you shocked or in awe? Or did you shrug your shoulders and think, "What's so special about them?"*

I used to work for the Dallas Morning News in the ads department, and every so often we would have several of the Dallas Cowboys come through the building doing interviews. It was really nice seeing the football players. I noticed when they arrived I was glad to see them, but I was not ecstatic. Well one day it was rumored the actor Will Smith was in the building. I was a super-fan! So I hurriedly put my job on hold and raced to the elevator along with every other employee in the building in hopes of seeing him exit the building. Five minutes later the supervisors came to the lobby and told everyone to go back to their desks, but nobody moved! *LOL. I guess a chance to see Will Smith was worth getting fired!* Anyway, they urged us all the more, but still they got the same response, nobody moved. *Surprising, huh?!*

Soon they realized we were not budging so they escorted Will Smith from the elevators with thunderous applause! *But here's the catch!* I wasn't as enthused with being in the presence of the football players because I've played football my entire life. However, being in the presence of Will Smith was a totally new experience for me.

In addition to my own excitement, I saw that

same spirit of anticipation and exhilaration began to swell as the crowd continued to gather! I saw some women putting on make-up, others combing their hair, and a few taking off their flats and putting on their heels. I also saw some men buttoning their shirts, tucking in their shirt tails, and trying to look their best.

Then it hit me! They were making sure they were presentable before they met Will Smith! Now if a person will go through all that to receive a famous man, how far will you go to make sure you receive Christ the right way? Besides, If I can run to get a chance to take a photo-op with Will Smith, I better be ready to do much more when I meet Christ!

Just In Case We Meet The Lord!

When I left the small town country life for the bright lights of the big city and college at eighteen, I was a bucket of nerves. When I arrived at Sam Houston State for fall two-a-day football practice, I was blessed to quickly discover I had an older cousin on the football team named Bobby Jr. Durham and he immediately took me under his wing. On the football field Bobby was strong and fast and he played the game with reckless abandon. Away from the football field, especially on the interstate, Bobby drove like he played football. *It's a contact sport!*

Bobby, who's now a Dallas Police Officer, used to drive a two-door Chevy Impala Super Sport and he only had one speed: *warp speed!* As we traveled on the interstate it seemed the two lane highway would instantly become Bobby's playground. While I was nervous of his driving around Huntsville, I was downright terrified when we drove through Houston!

It seemed to me the more congested the traffic, the more Bobby's speed demon would come out. I personally think he heard, *"Go speed racer,"* every time we entered Houston traffic. It was like the interstate became his own private Indy 500; and since I was his wing man, I was along for the ride no matter how it ended! Till this day I know, beyond a shadow of a doubt, that God spared us on multiple occasions. With Bobby dodging semi's and zig-zagging around Houston's interstate construction it's a miracle we made it out alive!

One faithful day Bobby had decided to *go where no man had gone before* as we traveled at light speed through downtown Houston. I was braced for the collision! In my terror I was trying to make my entire body recede from the front seat to the back by pressing my feet against the floor board with every near miss! Then for some reason I cast a terrified eye over at Bobby and I was flabbergasted to see he was *actually* laughing! I mean he looked like the Joker from Batman as he laughed and dodged semis, but the scariest part of this whole experience was noticing that during the entire time he was holding a Bible in his lap!

Later when my heart rate returned to normal, I asked him why he was holding the Bible. He responded, "Just in case we meet the Lord!"

Wow! Since you are reading this book it's safe to assume we did not meet the Lord on that day or any of our other subsequent starship enterprise treks as we traveled across space and time. But every time Bobby started cackling and I saw that gleam in his eye, I knew what was coming next. He'd start reaching for that Bible. Then one day out of the blue it came to me; I thought, *"What good will just holding it do? Shouldn't we know what's on the inside?* I mean especially if we are preparing ourselves to meet the Lord?"

Consider this, just holding a Bible or having it in your possession doesn't make you Holy. Actually, it just makes you a person holding a Bible. But, if you take the Word, read it and apply it to your life, you will discover that the words will transfer from the pages of the Bible and become written on your heart. That's why Psalms 119:11 says, *"I have hidden Your word in my heart that I might not sin against You."*

Understand just holding a Bible does not make you Holy. Nor does having a Bible placed in your living room sanctify your home. *If anything, having a Bible in your presence but not in your heart can make you more rebellious, haughty and your spirit untamable because you are trusting in the book and not the God of the book.* The Bible is no more than cow skin wrapped around leaflets of paper, but when you *read* and *understand* the words it contains, the Word of God will come alive in you, and you will see and receive Him for who He is and not who you *think* He is.

This is why the Centurion could say, "Speak and Word" and have faith based results while Jairus was forced to say, "Come to my house." The Centurion knew he was addressing the Son of God. Jairus Didn't. If Jairus knew who he was speaking to he could have asked for Christ to "speak a word," and it would have saved him a lot of unnecessary anguish and pain.

Do you think part of Jairus's problem was he didn't know how to see Christ? Do you think he was looking through the wrong lens? Do you think he saw Jesus like many see the bible? To Jairus Jesus was something to keep around for emergencies, but he was unwilling to take the time to discover the true value of what's inside the container of Jesus Christ.

Remember, when Christ came in human form he came as one of no reputation. (Philippians 2:6-7)

So there was nothing "extra" about Christ that would draw extra attention to Himself. Jesus was not covered in the latest "bling" or fashioned suit. The text says he came as a bond servant so that if people looked at the cover only, they would miss the true gift that was contained inside.

Who Touched Me?

As Jairus begins leading Christ to his home, I believe the seas of people began to part around Jairus and Christ. *As they walked I see in my mind a God who looked like a natural man and a man that strived to look like God. Oh my, how looks can be deceiving!* I believe to some degree that in his troubled mind Jairus was use to this type of treatment. As a Synagogue official he was used to having people moving around him as he went along with his daily duties, but we must remember when we invite Christ into our hearts we give Him authority over our lives, which means *He can put us on pause whenever He deems it's necessary.*

What's the beauty of a "who touched me" pause? It builds our faith. If you are in need of a healing (as Jairus was,) but you don't possess the faith for that healing (as Jairus didn't), what's the best way to cause your faith to grow? By watching someone else receive their healing! Why does this work? Because when you witness someone receiving their healing, you begin to hope, which leads to your faith growing as you think, "If He can do it for them —He can do it for me!" (Hebrews 11:1)

As Jairus progressed through the crowd he was probably praying for people to move and get out of the way! However, somewhere between his meeting place *with Christ* and his destination *for Christ,* he hears the Master begin to speak to a woman who had an infirmity for twelve years and it *immediately* stopped his progress *in Christ, or so he thought.*

It's Called A Right Relationship

When Christ puts you on Pause your forward momentum might have ceased, but your spiritual growth is about to exponentially explode! See there IS joy when you're stuck on Pause! As the words "Who touched me?" passed through Christ's lips, it brought Jairus hope of a quick resolution for his daughters healing to a screeching halt! The reason for this cessation was due to a new dynamic being formed in their relationship. Jairus couldn't lead anymore. It was time to transition and establish a right relationship.

Before you can get your healing or your deliverance you must be willing to enter into a right-relationship with Christ.

Pastor Emeritus Dr C. Paul McBride taught me that all things are possible with God when we have a right relationship with the Lord. Being a Christian is like attending kindergarten. All you have to do is listen to your teacher and follow the leader.

If you are on the pathway of faith, sooner or later you will experience a "who touched me" moment with God. *The reason for this is proper positioning must be established before any miracles can begin! The blessing of this moment is that it teaches us Christ is the leader and we are the follower.* When the woman with the issue of blood touched Jesus Jairus' was *immediately* placed on pause. For many of us we would naturally desire to throw some kind of fit! Frustrations, anger, disappointment, fear, and rage would all be natural responses to this situation. I mean Jesus was coming to the house right? He was onboard, right? But *now* we have to stop and wait for Him to deal with this old woman?

When you read the text you'll see the statement "Who touched me?" comes after the woman with the issue of blood was already healed! So why the statement? Remember Christ knew all things! So he knew who touched Him. This line of questioning was solely for Jairus' benefit so he could witness her healing, and it caused his faith to grow. Remember, faith comes by seeing and hearing the Word of God. Who is the Word? Christ Jesus! (Romans 10:17).

In this moment Jairus is forced to have a front row seat and watch someone else receive a healing he wished he had for his daughter! In their entire discourse of Christ dealing with the woman with the issue of blood Jairus never said a word! When God is building your faith, communication goes out the window because you are there as a witness and witnesses never testify while the miracle is happening. They testify of the miracle later.

This pause in Jairus' life was a faith building exercise to teach him two main things. First, it was to show him what true faith looked like as he watched this woman risk death to touch Christ. Second, when proper positioning is established, blessings automatically begin to flow.

In this *"Who touched me?"* moment is the entrance to understanding *The Joy of being Stuck on Pause*. The *"Who touched me"* moment is somewhat bittersweet because it gives us the time and opportunity to realize we do not have control, He does. Remember we are in agreement with Christ so we must have a "not my will but thy will be done" attitude. If Christ says *"Wait"* we must wait. If Christ says *"Go"* we must go.

Jairus thought he was leading Christ, but with Christ's stopping on the way to his house, it forced Jairus to stop as well. How could Jairus continue without Christ? Simply put he couldn't. Christ is the only one who could heal his daughter. So he was forced to wait on the Lord.

Can you fix your marriage? Can you resurrect the dead? No, none of us can. So it's best for us to wait on Christ and let Him work this out for us. I believe Jairus came to this understanding while he watched this woman be delivered of her illness. I believe he understood that to try and continue on would break fellowship with Christ and would cost him the life of his daughter.

So do you want to walk on without Christ? That isn't a wise decision. When Christ asked the twelve disciples if they wanted to leave Him in John 6:67-69 Peter said, "Lord, to whom shall we go? You have the words of eternal life."

Where can we go but to Jesus? *We have no choice but to wait on the Master because He is the only one who has healing power. Now it must be a hard thing for Jairus to wait for his healing, but this woman was also waiting for hers!*

This is why we can't become frustrated at those who come to Jesus or the order they come in. In Christ this woman's issue was just as important as Jairus'; the only difference is she decided to go get her blessing instead of waiting on it! Notice Christ made the church leader wait while he dealt with this sick woman who had nothing to do with church leadership. Actually, she wasn't even a church member because her disease forbade it!

Doesn't this tell us something about Christian leadership? Christ always blesses the sheep before he blesses the shepherd. However, in today's world the church seeks to bless the shepherd before we bless the sheep. There's something wrong with this picture.

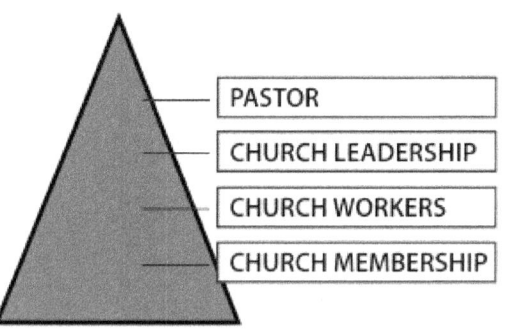

Many churches function like a pyramid with a downward power structure. The pastor holds the power in the church and he releases it as he sees fit. However this model oppresses the voice of the people.

Now let's look at the correct formula for the servant leader model.

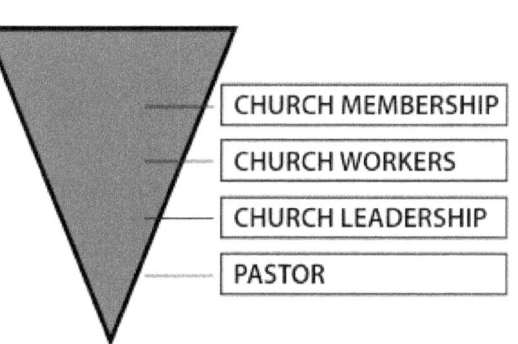

The true leadership model is with an upside down pyramid. The pastor "serves" the leaders who in turn "serve" the workers who in turn serve the membership. This is the Servant-Leader Model.

Which group needs the most *attention* in the church? Which group is the most *vulnerable* to the attack by the enemy? Which group will need the most support and care? Which group is most like a new born lamb? Yes, it is the church body. In this model the pastor, leaders, and church workers, all serve the church membership.

Some might say this is not fair for God to put Jairus on pause to deal with this woman with an issue of blood. Some might say he was there first, so he should be blessed first. Some might even say he was a preacher so he should get his blessing first because he had a higher calling on his life rather than some no-names pew member.

Aren't you glad our God does not work like that? This blessing teaches us whoever makes contact with Christ will be healed. The centurion touched Christ spiritually and this woman touched Him physically and both instantly received their healing. Jairus on the other hand remained dogmatic which caused his blessing to be delayed.

Please, do not miss this. Jairus worshiped God, entreated God, praised God, but he never *touched* God *spiritually or physically*. Not touching Christ when we have the opportunity puts us in an uncomfortable position when we see others get blessed.

The Pressure Of Seeing Others Get Blessed!

One of the hardest lessons for a Christian is to learn how to stand in faith while seeing others who come to Christ *after* you seem to be blessed *before* you. As Christians we *constantly* compare ourselves and our walk to other Christians. When we see them get blessed we instantly think, *"What's wrong with me? Why am I not being blessed?"* Instead of us thinking our pause is God's will, we instantly begin thinking we're not prospering because of sin.

For a person that's "doing all the right things in church," it's almost crippling to see someone that's new to the faith get a better job or promotion than the one we have, but that's not the mind of God nor should it be ours.

In today's world too many Christians are like the older brother of the prodigal son. We work in the Fathers house and we do what He says, but as soon as we see Him blessing someone we think or feel is unworthy, we rebel against Him.

"Now his older son was in the field. And as he came and drew near to the house, he heard music and dancing. So he called one of the servants and asked what these things meant. And he said to him, 'Your brother has come, and because he has received him safe and sound, your father has killed the fatted calf.' "But he was angry and would not go in.

Therefore his father came out and pleaded with him." (Luke 15: 25-28)

Notice what the scriptures say about the oldest son. There are several things that stand out. The oldest son looks to be a mature child of God. Notice we find him out in the father's field working for his Lord, but just because he has a job doesn't mean he was *thankful* for his employment or *mature* in his employment.

But isn't this what all saved and righteous children of God should be doing for their Father? Shouldn't we be working in the Father's field, because His field is really our field?

I am a country boy that grew up tending to my parents farm. The years of hauling hay, working cows, and fixing fences has made me into a very hard working person. In my youth the daily grind of farm life taught me I needed to get an education because at the time I did not want to do it, but now it shows me how valuable my labor was. I remember when I was immature I worked the farm because my father told me so. However, when I matured he told me one day the farm would pass from his hands to me and my brother.

Knowing that I had a workable part of the farm meant a lot to me, and I keep that in mind to this day. I know that no matter what I do with my life, I have a responsibility to the farm and my parents to keep it up and make sure I take care of it. This is my duty as a son and an heir because one day it will pass from me to my children.

Because of his reaction to his brother's homecoming party, I believe somewhere along the way this elder brother lost sight of the fact that although he was working in his Father's field, he was receiving blessings from his labor. After a long day of working, *before arriving at his Father's house*, he is greeted by music and loud voices. Do you think he was surprised by this?

Why would a child of God be shocked and surprised by a party in His Father's House? What do you think we're going to do when we get to Heaven? Sit around and be sad? No! We're going to party with Jesus!

Furthermore, it shouldn't be a shock to us that our backslidden brothers and sisters come home. *Chances are we've been in a backslidden state once or twice in our ministry journey as well.* Jeremiah 3: 14 say's, *"Return, O backsliding children,"* says the LORD; *"for I am married to you."* With this in mind shouldn't we be thankful that God has blessed us to be a part of His family and that every brother and sister who comes back to God is a testimony of His goodness and grace?

As we continue to examine the mindset of the older brother, we discover his intentions were not honorable and he was making fleshly decisions. The scripture says *"So he called one of the servants and asked what these things meant."* It's sad to see this older brother operating in a bad attitude. Why didn't he go see His Father? Why ask a servant when you have a right relationship with God?

When we understand that we can go straight to the source, we begin to ascertain that there's no reason to go to the servant or any other mediator! So there is no need for us to go to a servant for information from God; we can go to the source. So how should we approach God? With Boldness knowing He wants to talk to you! The Bible says in Hebrews 4:6, *"Let us therefore come boldly to the throne of grace that we may obtain mercy and find grace to help in time of need."*

The reaction of the older, supposing more mature brother, is quite surprising, especially when he finds out his immature brother comes home *and has been restored.* The text says, *"And he said to him, 'Your brother has come, and because he has received him safe and sound, your father has killed the fatted calf.' "But he was angry and would not go in. Therefore his father came out and pleaded with him."*

Personally, I don't believe that the older brother cared if his younger brother came back, but I do believe he thought he should have been made a servant instead of a son. But notice the Father would not allow His son to be devalued. The Father received His son back the same way as when he left —as a child of the King. Even the prodigal son expected to be downgraded from a son to a servant, but the father would have none of it. When the servant told the older brother, *"He has received him safe and sound,"* it triggered the downward plunge of his character.

Many of us think the blessing of the Father is the fatted calf, but who cares if the calf is killed? You still don't have the right relationship with God! Do we need to cover the mindset of Cain again?

How do you know if you have this mindset or not? Your self-righteousness will keep you out of the house. *"But he was angry and would not go in. Therefore his father came out and pleaded with him." Sometimes when we're stuck on pause and we see others getting blessed, it causes the ugliness within our souls to come out.*

For many of us this is our greatest challenge when we're on pause. Can you stand to see someone else get blessed? Can you stand shouting over someone's deliverance from drugs knowing your child is hooked or strung out? Can you praise God for His restoring someone's marriage while yours is falling apart? Can you praise Him when you're at a spiritual standstill and it seems that everyone else is passing you by?

What Do You Mean "Thousands"?

Jealousy in ministry is a dangerous thing. Jealousy will make a vexing spirit rise up in a person, and it will allow them to do unspeakable things to another child of God. We see this in the relationship between Cain with Abel, Saul and David, and finally Judas with Jesus. Each of these relationships shows us how easily relationships can sour because of pride and jealousy.

The disintegration of the relationship between Saul and David was not over land, money, or the crown. It was based on a single compliment.

In the beginning of their relationship Saul and David seemed like a match made in Heaven. I Samuel 16: 21-23 says, *"David came to Saul and stood before him. And he loved him greatly, and he became his armor bearer. Then Saul sent to Jesse, saying, "Please let David stand before me, for he has found favor in my sight." And so it was, whenever the spirit from God was upon Saul, that David would take a harp and play it with his hand. Then Saul would become refreshed and well, and the distressing spirit would depart from him."*

When we take a closer look at this text we see that Saul loved David, but he did not love him for who he was. He loved him for how he made him feel. When the evil spirit came upon Saul David played music for him, and it soothed Saul's soul.

This *"false love"* becomes evident in I Samuel 18:6-9 and the warm and fuzzy feelings Saul had for David quickly turned into jealousy and hatred. The text says, "A*s they were coming home, when David was returning from the slaughter of the Philistine, that the women had come out of all the cities of Israel, singing and dancing, to meet King Saul, with tambourines, with joy, and with musical instruments. So the women sang as they danced, and said:" Saul has slain his thousands, And David his ten thousands." Then Saul was very angry, and the saying displeased him; and he said, 'They have ascribed to David ten thousands, and to me they have ascribed only thousands. Now what more can he have but the kingdom?' So Saul eyed David from that day forward."*

When Saul heard this awesome compliment being attributed to David *instead of him* it caused his feelings towards David to change and his fondness became a mixture of jealousy, fear, and hatred. Perhaps Saul viewed himself as a ladies' man? Maybe Saul wanted all the kudos from the victory? Or maybe Saul didn't want to share any of the glory? I believe Saul saw himself as little in his own eyes (I Samuel 15:17) and he couldn't handle seeing someone else get blessed.

It's a sad thing to see a father in ministry become jealous of the son he promoted then strive to kill their character and spirit!

Now did David do or say anything wrong? No, he didn't. Scripture says in I Samuel 18:14, *"David behaved wisely in all his ways, and the Lord was with him."* David never wronged Saul nor did he bring disgrace to Saul, but because of this minor compliment, it caused major issues between Saul and David. When you look at David's military record as he served Saul, you'll see David protected him, blessed him, ministered to him, and even killed a giant for him. *So how did Saul choose to repay his faithful servant? He repeatedly tried to kill David.*

Do you think this is the spirit of the older brother in the parable of the prodigal son? Do you see the older brother wanted the praise because of his hard work in the field? Do you want praise from people because of *your* work in ministry? Do you think the older brother was only concerned with his "thousands? Or do you think he saw his brother's homecoming as if he was receiving "ten thousands?" Simply put, are you *little* in your own eyes?

True the younger brother had gone off and lived a physically corrupt lifestyle, but the older brother was living a spiritually corrupt life, and as long as his brother didn't come home he never would have known it! So maybe he should have been thankful because his brother's presence showed him an area within himself he needed to address.

I have discovered people who are "little in their

own eyes" are people who need a title. They need and desire the title or constant recognition because it gives them the boost they feel they need to be accepted. The title brother or sister in Christ isn't enough. They call themselves "preachers" but they've never been licensed. They call themselves "pastors or bishops," but they've never overseen a church; yet they seek the applause of men to make them feel good about themselves instead of valuing the only title that counts: Child of God.

Many Christians are just like Saul and this older brother. They don't want to share the praise. They want it all for themselves. This constitutes sins of the spirit. I'm sure during the younger brother's absence the older brother had all the *fatted calf* he could eat! But no matter how much he ate, he was still unwilling to share with his brother.

What is it that causes many of us to be jealous while God is blessing someone else? This is the reason many of us are on pause. We are so concerned with what God is giving to others that it stops Him from giving (blessings) into our lives. Can you imagine such a noble and wonderful occasion as a lost saint coming back into the House of God but *we* refuse to come into God's house because we hate seeing our brothers blessed and restored?

Saints, it's a sad day when we can't shout when someone

else gets blessed.

In the mindset of many people who find themselves on pause there is usually a struggle to find their own righteousness in God. It says, *"Hey, why is Christ healing and blessing everyone else while I am I stuck on pause? Here I am; I'm paying my tithes, I'm coming to church, I'm fasting, I'm praying, I'm there at Bible study, why am I put on hold? The very people who come to Christ last seem like they get the best blessings first! Why am I put on hold? Why am I struggling for so long?*

The Waiting Game

I can see your mind twirling and asking me, *"Well preacher, this is a good lesson, but just how long is my pause? How long will I have to watch others precede me in getting blessed?"*

Well let's look at the Prophet Ezekiel and see how long it took him to fulfill *one* of his missions in God. In Ezekiel 4:1-6 it says, *"This will be a sign to the house of Israel. Lie also on your left side, and lay the iniquity of the house of Israel upon it. According to the number of the days that you lie on it, you shall bear their iniquity. For I have laid on you the years of their iniquity, according to the number of the days, three hundred and ninety days; so you shall bear the iniquity of the house of Israel."*

Imagine, here is one of the most radical prophets of the Old Testament being reduced to a mannequin for the glorious name of God. Can you imagine the conversation between Ezekiel and God? I'm sure it went something like, *"Ezekiel, I need to teach my people a lesson and you are my living testimony. So every day for 390 days I want you to get up come outside and build a replica of Israel. Then lie down on your side all day as a sign to the people. Yes, folk are going to walk by you and talk about you, but I want you to lie there. You can't get up, you can't move, you can't talk to them nor address them in any way. Your ministry for the next 390 days is to simply lie there and don't move."*

Do you think you can do it? I have to admit it would have been hard for me too! 390 days straight! No weekends or time off! God didn't allow any sick days for Ezekiel and at the end of the trial God said, *"Now flip over to your right side and lie there forty additional days for Judah."*

When this trial was complete God said, *"Now Ezekiel, this one is going to hurt. My children haven't learned their lesson, so I'm going to take the apple of your eye. I'm going to take your wife. Don't even run home because she's going to be dead by the time you get there anyway."* He says, *"Now you're going to have to suffer, but you can't weep, Ezekiel. You can't cry, you can't mourn your wife because you're my example and the pain and suffering the Israelites see you going through is an exact replica of how they treat Me."* (Ezekiel

24:16-18 paraphrase).

Can you imagine the pain that Ezekiel went through? When the people finally came to Ezekiel and questioned him about why God laid such a heavy burden on him, God said, *"Ezekiel is a sign to you; according to all that he has done you shall do; and when this comes, you shall know that I am the Lord God."(Ezekiel 24:24).*

Let's talk about another man of God who had to wait for an extended amount of time. In a single afternoon Job lost everything. He lost all of his possessions and his family. Five hundred yoke of oxen and five hundred donkeys carried off by Sabeans, seven thousand sheep burned up by the fire of God which fell from the sky, three thousand camels stolen and the house of the firstborn collapsed killing all of Job's offspring. In spite of all this Job did not curse God but he said, *"Naked I came out of my mother's womb, and naked shall I return: Lord has given, and Lord has taken away; blessed be the name of Lord."* (Job 1:21)

It's almost mind boggling that Job had to endure so much before he was stuck on pause. So how long did Job wait? Thirty eight chapters. That's how long it took Job to get a right relationship with God and the wisdom to pray for his friends so that his captivity turned into a celebration. (Job 42:10)

When you are in need it is hard to wait on God; however, the things that befell Job *before* he had to wait on God were catastrophic. Even after losing so much and then having Satan attack his body with painful boils and sores to the point he had to scratch himself with a broken pot shard, Job never sinned against God. He simply sat in an area surrounding the town trash dump for seven days of silence. When he spoke he cursed the day he was born, but he never cursed God. When his friends accused him of sinful living Job said in chapter 13:15, *"Though He slay me, yet will I trust Him."* And in chapter 14:14 he said, *"If a man dies, shall he live again? All the days of my hard service I will wait, till my change comes."* Now that's a man that understands there's a purpose in his pause.

Study Guide

Chapter 4: Uh, Jesus? – I'm Stuck!

1. Have you ever had a "Just In Case We Meet The Lord!" moment in ministry? What did that moment teach you about your relationship with God? If you met Him today would you have a right relationship or a wrong relationship? Why or why not?

2. Have you taken time to "touch God" today? Why or why not? Why is it important to touch God? Jairus was in close proximity to the Master but he never sought to touch Christ. Do you know of any person in your present or past that had the opportunity to touch Christ but they refused? Share your thoughts.

3. As you looked at the servant leader model, what does this chart tell you about the ministry you serve? Is your church focused on making the membership its main concentration or the pastor? Do you believe this is a good model? Why or why not?

4. Imagine you have to stand on the sideline and watch others get blessed. How would it make you feel? If you were waiting on a healing for years would it make you frustrated or angry to see a new believer cured from the very disease you are dealing with? Why or why not?

5. When you see that Ezekiel and Job had to wait an extended time, how does that make you feel towards you own pauses? Do you think it's better to rebel against God and bog yourself down, or do you think you should try to patiently wait for God to deliver you? Why or why not?

CHAPTER 5

Walk With Me, Lord!

While He was still speaking, some came from the ruler of the synagogue's house who said, "Your daughter is dead. Why trouble the Teacher any further?" As soon as Jesus heard the word that was spoken, He said to the ruler of the synagogue, "Do not be afraid; only believe and she will be made well."
~Luke 8:49-50

Faith isn't the ability to believe long and far into the misty future. It's simply taking God at His Word and taking the next step.
~ Joni Erickson Tada

Growing up in small Baptist churches in East Texas we learned all manner of gospel songs. One of my favorites that still move me today is a song entitled

"*Walk with me, Lord.*" Here are the lyrics:

> *Walk with me Lord; walk with me,*
> *Walk with me Lord; walk with me,*
> *While I'm on this tedious journey,*
> *I want Jesus to walk with me.*

I remember while I was growing up I would often hear my mother singing this song repeatedly while she was cooking in the kitchen. At the time I had no idea what a "tedious journey" was, but the longer I stay on this walk of Grace I understand it more and more. The word tedious simply implies something that is long and tiresome.

If you've ever been on a long trip you've experienced this feeling. Early in our marriage there were several times Brenda and I had to travel from Dallas to California for family visits. Since we were newlyweds and money was tight, we had to drive instead of fly, and let me tell you *that* was a tedious journey!

Typically this journey takes twenty-two to twenty-four hours. In our haste to get to California, as quickly as possible, we would drive straight through to California while pausing only long enough to get snacks or for restroom breaks. With us trying to accomplish so much in such a small amount of time there was no time for enjoyment or sightseeing. No matter the weather or traffic conditions we just had to keep it pushing until we reached our destination.

When you add in two young children in diapers, the trip became excruciating. During the trips they constantly cried because they were strapped in car seats with little to no movement. Brenda did the best she could by trying to play with them and keep their spirits up, but even the best mom would crack under that kind of pressure. As we traveled down that long dark highway I remember I kept thinking *"Lord, when will this tedious journey end?"*

Over time I learned to appreciate the bright lights of the cities that we travelled through as they served to break the monotony of the desert travel. It seemed that each city was a pleasant oasis of life and excitement instead of the wastelands of the deserts and open plains we traveled through. Whenever we would leave each city I would get a bit sad because I knew I had miles upon miles of empty space ahead of me.

Sometimes the walk of Christ is like that trip to California. You experience tedious seasons; you will feel like it's been an eternity since you've seen any happiness or sunshine in your life.

Whenever I think about those long trips, I have to say I am always thankful for Brenda. Mile upon mile she did her best to keep me encouraged and focused on my task of driving. Whenever I would start to tire, she would step right in by handing me snacks or drinks to lift me up, changing the music to encourage me, or just offering great conversation to keep awake with my mind on our priorities. With her by my side we always made great time and we always arrived safely.

But even Brenda got tired and every so often her eyes would get droopy and she would fall asleep leaving me to face those long miles alone. But it didn't take me long to discover that I had someone that I could talk to and travel with even when Brenda and the kids fell asleep.

The second time we drove to California we encountered a violent sand storm that left us in total darkness. Brenda and the kids were asleep, but in a desire to get to California I kept driving a break neck speed although I couldn't see three feet in front of my window. That's when I heard the soothing voice of the Lord say "Ray, slow down. You can't see." Knowing that was God's voice, I instantly began to decrease my speed until I was barely at a crawl. No sooner than I decreased my speed to less than five miles an hour, I saw a *parked* car in front of me on the interstate, just two feet ahead.

Apparently the driver in front of me couldn't

see either so instead of driving forward he decided to stop in the middle of the interstate and wait for the storm to pass. If I had kept driving at the eighty miles an hour speed I was traveling, I would have crashed into the back of their car probably killing everybody in both cars. That was when I learned that Jesus was walking with us on that tedious journey the entire time, and the whole time He was silent until I needed Him most.

Learn To Walk With God

We as individuals, ministries, and churches must learn to walk with God. Although this sounds easy, it really isn't. It takes time on this Christian journey to mature to where you learn to bless those that curse you and continuously try to use you. If it wasn't for the mandate of Christ, many of us would bypass this command in a second. Christ said in Luke 6: 27-28, *"But I say to you who hear: Love your enemies, do good to those who hate you, bless those who curse you, and pray for those who spitefully use you."*

When I was injured playing football the damage to my knee was so catastrophic; I had to relearn how to walk not once but twice. One second I was a pretty decent college football player, and in the next,

I was labeled handicapped by my doctor with a parking sticker to boot. The two torn ligaments and dead nerve in my right knee permanently sidelined me and for the next eighteen months I lived on crutches. Countless hours of rehab plus two major knee operations in that time span had my life reeling.

The first time I had to relearn how to walk was with a brace right after my initial injury. I remember hating the looks I received from people staring at the awkwardness of how I walked. The second time I had to relearn how to walk was ten years later, but by that time I didn't care who stared because Jesus had converted my soul and the awkwardness of my walk gave me the opportunity to testify of God's faithfulness to someone like me.

The first time I tried walking without my crutches brought about a horrific moment in my life. It was probably a week after my surgery; I was in my bedroom at my apartment and I wanted to get a drink of water. I knew I couldn't put all my weight on my injured leg so I decided to hop to the kitchen. As I began the process of hopping across the dark room, I stepped on something sharp with my left foot and instantly switched my weight to my damaged leg without thinking. Immediately my entire right leg felt like fire! It was as if metal bands of heat grabbed my left side. Excruciating pain seized my body as it resonated throughout my entire being.

I instantly crumbled to the floor clutching my knee from the pain and all thought vanished. I clamped my teeth and turn my face towards the carpeted floor to stifle the scream that was trying to press through my teeth. As the tears fell from my face, I slowly crawled back to my bed. When I was able, I pulled my body back onto my bed and rolled onto the sheets feeling pain, shame, and hurt because I tried to do something my body was not ready for.

Many of us experience this in the spiritual realm. We try to walk in God when we are not prepared, and more times than not we collapse under the weight of our trials because we lack the strength to endure the pain.

The walk of God is a process. All of us begin the same way, as babes in Christ. As we grow, the daily issues we face give our feeble child-like muscles exercise so they can build strength for the tests that are sure to come our way in God. I remember an old quote that said, *"What doesn't kill you makes you stronger."* In the spirit realm this is very true. We are called by God to *"wrestle against spiritual wickedness in high places."* To do this requires strong men and women of God, seasoned warriors, not immature saints who are willing to stand in their faith against these oppressive powers.

Spiritual growth is a process. We all begin by crawling. As we press towards maturity, we move from crawling to making teetering steps of faith in God, then walking in mature faith.

If there was anyone that walked with God and had a strong relationship with Him it would be Enoch. The Bible tells us in Genesis 5: 24, *"And Enoch walked with God; and he was not, for God took him."* Now that is a testimony!

One of my mentors recently said, "The key to a good sermon is to have a great beginning as well as a great ending, and keep them as close together as possible." Well if that is the case then Enoch "lived" a truly great sermon! He wasn't around long but he made a lasting impression on this Bible reader.

If you take a close look at Genesis 5, you will see a long list of Adam's children and how their lives were chronicled. The formula is very simple and basic. They lived, had children, and then they died. However, when it refers to Enoch it says "and he was not, for God took him."

Please understand Enoch did not die. God *translated* him. It's as if God moved Enoch from being a physical being to a spiritual being in an instant. It is almost as if God *changed* Enoch the same way He will *change* us on that great day of the rapture. (I Corinthians 15:51-53)

If our change will come within the "twinkling of an eye," then can't you see why Enoch's was as well? As you can tell, when God is ready for you to come home, I pray you are prepared because He moves fast.

Like all of us, Enoch was introduced to God somewhere along the path of his daily living. It was here God revealed Himself to Enoch. God met Moses on a mountain, Gideon by a winepress, and the three Hebrew boys in a furnace. *So needless to say, our God is terrific at knowing where and when He needs to introduce Himself.* Enoch could have met God during a church service or maybe He spoke to him while he was on his evening stroll. Either way scripture does not tell how they met; it only lets us know that from that meeting *Enoch walked with God.*

What does it take to walk with God? You first must decide to live a life of faith. We can't walk with God if we aren't going to live by His precepts. Hebrews 11:6 says, *"For he who comes to God must believe that He is, and that He is a rewarder of those who diligently seek Him."*

Then you must decide to be committed to the walk which means *continuously* submitting your will to His. God doesn't share headship or leadership. It's either you submit to His will or not. Paul said the role of the individual and the church is to mature spiritually in all things by being subject to our head which is Christ. (Ephesians 4:14-16)

Keep in mind learning to trust God is a process. It takes time and serious trials in our lives for us to hand over the decision making process to God.

When you trace his life, you see that according to Genesis 5: 21-24, *"Enoch lived sixty-five years, and begot Methuselah. After he begot Methuselah, Enoch walked with God three hundred years, and had sons and daughters. So all the days of Enoch were three hundred and sixty-five years. And Enoch walked with God; and he was not, for God took him."*

For the next few moments let's talk about *why* Enoch walked with God. When we look at the text we see several things that stand out about Enoch. Just like you and me Enoch's life held a B.C. (Before Christ) and his A.D. (After the Death of Christ.)

The scripture says, *"Enoch lived sixty-five years, and begot Methuselah."* How do we know this is Enoch's B.C.? We know this because there is no mention of God before the naming of his first born. However, after the birth of Methuselah the text immediately mentions, *"After he begot Methuselah, Enoch walked with God."(Genesis 5:24)*

As we begin to unpack this text, we see that something transpired between God and Enoch around the birth of his firstborn that had a significant enough effect that it affected the naming of his son. For sixty-five years Enoch lived an unsaved life. Like all of us he was born into sin. David echoed this same sentiment in Psalms 51:5. The text says, *"Behold,*

I was brought forth in iniquity, and in sin my mother conceived me."

Things changed when Christ began moving in his life. When we continue with the text it says, *"After he begot Methuselah, Enoch walked with God."* Here lies a very deep revelation of the spirit. Enoch's life, Jairus' life, my life, and your life all have a B.C., our Before Christ. However, somewhere in our lives God revealed Himself to us and from the moment we said, "Yes," to His will, we began operating in our A.D.

To dissect the revelation we must look at his son Methuselah. The Bible teaches us Enoch was converted after the birth of Methuselah. He was converted from the pagan worship of his day to being a child of Jehovah. God revealed a secret to Enoch when he was at the tender age of sixty- five that changed the entire direction of his life.

As many of us know Biblical names often refer to the character of the person or some attribute of God they possess. The name *Methuselah* carries two parts. The first part means *man-die,* and the second part signifies a dart as if it has been *thrown or sent.* A literal translation of the two components means *"when he dies it shall be sent."*

You may ask, *"What was sent the year after Methuselah's death that Enoch was able to see by being connected to God?"* It was the flood in Genesis 6.

In the book of Numbers 14:18 Moses writes this testimony about God. He says, *"The Lord is longsuffering and abundant in mercy, forgiving iniquity and transgression; but He by no means clears the guilty, visiting the iniquity of the fathers on the children to the third and fourth generation."* If you continue down the lineage of Enoch you will see four generations of sons. The lineage goes from Enoch, Methuselah, Lamech, and Noah. These four men all carried a singular purpose of walking with God. Although they were surrounded by all types of devil worship, they stood before God and they were instrumental in reestablishing creation after the flood.

This is the secret God shared with Enoch. God showed Enoch a vision for his family and Enoch raised his sons and daughters in the admonition of the Lord. This is why he named his first born Methuselah.

Methuselah lived 969 years. He, according to the Bible, was the longest living person on the planet. This is a testimony to God's love and His everlasting kindness. Even though He knew he was going to bring the flood onto mankind, he gave them close to a thousand years to repent. This is why the Bible teaches us in II Peter 3:8 *"Do not forget this one thing that with the Lord one day is as a thousand years, and a thousand years as one day."*

In Genesis 5:29 we see Lamech spoke a

prophecy over Noah. The text says, *"And he called his name Noah, saying, "This one will comfort us concerning our work and the toil of our hands, because of the ground which the LORD has cursed."*

This prophecy of Lamech was the *fulfillment* and *payment* of the sin-debt that began with Adam and Eve in the Garden. Although God allowed time to pass, the answer to how God deals with sin was found in Enoch, the seventh son of Adam. This message was delivered from Enoch down to the fourth generation of Noah and fulfilled in the outpouring of the flood.

This is the word of prophecy that God spoke to Enoch. God shared this word with him, and it converted his family and saved mankind in the form of an ark. My question to you is what word has God spoken to you that is for your family? What are you supposed to share with your children in your remaining years before you are called home? What vision are you supposed to write down for them so that they can run into their future and not be weary or faith? You never know. Maybe all of mankind can be blessed through your family the same way we are blessed through Enoch. All you have to do is choose this day if you will walk with God.

The reason we must walk closely with God is simple. The negative issues of life are designed to do one or two things.

They will either draw you closer to Christ or they will push you further away.

During this deliverance service of the woman with the issue of blood, Jairus is stuck on pause. He can't go forward and he can't go backwards. All he can do is wait on God. As the conversation between Christ and this woman came to the end, I can only imagine that his spirits began to soar because he felt he *still* had time. His daughter was *still* sick and he could *still* hold onto the fact that Christ can *still* heal her. In spite of his high hopes, as this conversation is ending, he sees a servant running from his house and he knows this *has got to be* bad news.

Why Trouble The Teacher, Anymore?

"Your daughter is dead. Why trouble the teacher, anymore?" Can you hear these words resonate in Jairus ears and down to his very soul? I mean he had come so far in such a short amount of time, but this is the blessedness of being on a tedious journey. You still have God with you! As Psalms 46:1 teaches us, *"God is our refuge and strength, a very present help in trouble."*

If there is anytime we need the presence of God surrounding us on the walk of life, it's when death has invaded *our ranks.*

Isaiah 40:29 says, *"He gives power to the weak, And to those who have no might He increases strength."* Saints, who can have strength when they have just learned their child is dead? Not me, nor you. But here Isaiah shows us when we are spent, empty, weak, or broken, God will give us the strength we need just to keep moving.

When I received the call of my grandmother's death, I was in college and it took all my energy just to hang up the phone. As I sat on the corner of the bed in my dorm room, I hung my head and cried. Once my tears stopped flowing, I found I was still crying inside my heart and I knew in that moment it was a wound that would never close. As my head hung down all I could think to myself was, *"Keep breathing, keep breathing, and keep breathing."*

Sometimes life hits you right in the pit of your stomach and you might feel as if you're about to lose it, but if you can just "keep breathing," He will bring you out! When we are in need of God's power, strength, and helping hand, He stands ready to provide it. When Abraham proved to God he loved the Lord more than Isaac, God provided a Ram in the bush for his sacrifice. From that day forward Abram called that particular spot on the mountain Jehovah Jireh which translates to The Lord Will Provide. (Genesis 22:14)

The Psalmist said the Lord is a refuge (Psalms 46:11). Do you think Jairus needed the Lord to be a refuge for him? Can you perceive or sense how badly he needed Jesus with how *quickly* Christ dispelled the words of the servant? Christ knew He needed to be a refuge for Jairus because in that moment Jairus was truly broken.

For my purpose of writing it would be easy to paint this message delivered from the servant of Jairus as an act of the enemy, but that does not play true to the text. Although the servant knew who Christ was, we apparently see this in how he addresses Christ, he simply gave bad advice. *Sometimes Christians don't say the right things at the right time.* When we hear advice like *"leave the church, divorce your husband, or quit your job,"* it can come from someone that has our best interests at heart but can't see the full picture of how God is working things out for our good.

The statement, *"Why trouble the teacher any longer?"* is a statement to cause you to move away from Christ when in all actuality you need to move towards Christ. When we are in our most vulnerable spiritual states, we must always seek to come closer to the master.

Proverbs 18:10 says, *"The name of the LORD is a strong tower; the righteous run to it and are safe."* When you are in a never ending trial and it seems to only grow worse and worse, remember the Lord is a strong tower. Meaning, He is something that can't be breached by the attacks of the enemy. He is strong!

But keep this in mind; only the righteous can run into Him and be safe. There is no room for the unrighteous. So remember if you are on the pathway of God and you are following Christ, this is an open door for you! If the trial or test becomes too rough, run into the Master and you will find rest for your soul.

The Ministry In The Message

Keep in mind Jairus had made it through so much, but no sooner than Christ ends His conversation with this woman the report of his daughter's death comes *and he loses hope as his fear begins to creep in.*

It's here that we must figure out which message we will believe. Will it be the message of Faith or the message of Fear? When we are in a moment of shock and disbelief as Jairus was, we have two choices. We are going to believe in God, or we will believe in the facts of the situation.

The Bible dictionary defines fear as a natural feeling of alarm caused by the expectation of danger, pain, or disaster. However, Christ gives us freedom *from* fear as men and women put their faith in the Lord God who protects (Psalms 23:4) and helps (Isaiah 54:14) them through their physical and spiritual trials.

In these few seconds of Pause, Christ is speaking a word of Faith while the servant is speaking a word of Fear. But I praise God because Jairus choose to follow the voice of Christ rather than the voice of the servant.

Sometimes it can be hard to hear and discern the voice of God when you have multiple voices speaking in your head. *Now I am not assuming you are crazy!* But sometimes our fear, doubts, and insecurities speak to us; and when these are loosed in our minds, it can cause a tremendous uproar. That's why I am thankful that the voice of Christ will always *rise* above any distracting thought or voice.

This brief text lets us know that we must always seek to be in a position where we can hear the voice of Christ. *This is why location, location, location is so important!* The closer we are to Christ the louder His voice will speak within our spirit. The further away we are the less we can hear His voice.

Walking with God in the midst of death is a very hard thing. Sometimes you have to roll yourself up into a tight ball of belief and hold onto it for dear life. However it is in moments like these that our faith is truly tested. It is in times like these when we finally see a direct word spoken from Christ to Jairus where he simply said, *"Do not be afraid; only believe, and she will be made well."*

Throughout this text I find it ironic that Luke

surmised all of the conversation except this brief phrase. Is it because this short text is so important? As a man who did not walk with Christ but received his information from eye-witness testimony of the power of Christ, we see He took meticulous care to make sure he penned this few words correctly.

Notice how He specifically points to our fears? What is it about our fears that cancel our faith?

Christ in his first *direct* words to Jairus is giving a word of encouragement that seems hard for him to receive in this moment of death. Christ said, *"Do not be afraid."* Now we know that fear is the first cousin to anxiety, worry, doubt and concern. Rampant fear is the one spirit that cancels faith when we begin to move forward in life. It is a killer of your faith because for *faith to operate it must be unrestrained while fear seeks to restrain*. Because Jairus is with Christ there is very little he can go on, so he has to hold onto his faith.

This is where every step, no matter how big or small, is a victory in Jesus' Name.

But there is a special significance in this moment with Christ. Only He has resurrection power. Only Christ has the authority and will to bring this child back to life. Notice that while this child was still living, Jairus was on pause; but as soon as she was able to slip past his belief structure, he had to learn to operate in faith.

Here's another glorious revelation of the spirit. When we begin to walk in faith it immediately removes us from our Pause.

Remember he wanted Christ to come to the house, lay hands on her, and she would recover. This was while she was alive. What can he do now that she was dead? His only option was to believe! See Jairus had to come to realize that his last option was his only option and this is exactly where Christ wanted him to be.

As long as his daughter was still living Jairus operated in a mixture of fear, belief, and doubt, seeing the healing operate in only one way; but when she died his only recourse was to believe in Jesus Christ. This is why we have to be thankful when God allows death to enter our ranks because her death provided the jolt Jairus needed, and it forced him to focus on the only opinion that counted.

The Problem Of Having Two Opinions

The problem with having two opinions is you can't make any progress. If a person can't make a decision *and stick with it,* he is left to constantly travel backwards and forwards over the *"what if's"* in his mind and nothing will ever get done. This was a problem for Jairus and it was a big one with the Children of Israel. Throughout their history they couldn't seem to decide which God to follow. Will you follow the god of this world, Satan, or the God over Heaven and Earth, Jesus Christ? In 1 Kings 18:21 Elijah told the people, *"How long will you falter between two opinions? If the LORD is God, follow Him; but if Baal, follow him."* But the people answered him not a word."

During this time the people of God had become so intertwined with satanic worship that they didn't even know how to answer Elijah's question. They knew that Jehovah is the One that delivered them from bondage and preceded them in the Promised Land. However, they discovered Baal worship and chose to worship a heathen god through the sensuality of their flesh, and it led them back into a new type of bondage.

So through Elijah we discover they were being *forced* to make a decision: Were they going to follow God or Baal? Notice God did not try to force the Israelites to serve Him. He just told them through Elijah to make up their minds.

Forcing you to choose Christ is not our God's way of doing things. He won't force you. Remember you have to open the door of your heart to Him and allow Him to come in. But one thing Christ will not suffer is a child of God that's happy living between two opinions.

Sooner or later you have to make a decision or He'll make you make a decision.

As the old folks say, *"A man that straddles a fence will sooner or later develop a sore crouch!"* When Christ condemned the Laodicea church, He said in Revelation 3:14-15, *""I know your works, that you are neither cold nor hot. I could wish you were cold or hot. So then, because you are lukewarm, and neither cold nor hot, I will vomit you out of My mouth."*

Now that's a billboard sign that no church wants! "Come visit us! We are the church that made God sick!"

Can you imagine the depth of sin these people were in? They had lived a life of depravity for so long they refused to answer the prophet of the Lord. Saints, it is sad when we refuse to answer the call of our sin. But this is what the longevity of sin does to us. It dulls our senses to the point we openly defy God by supporting the evil He condemns, and that means we are living between two opinions.

We defy Him because we want to do "other than." We want our cake and eat it too! Inevitably, we want to fulfill the desires of our flesh and desires of our spirit simultaneously. But that's not how God operates.

These people knew God as Jehovah, but they were not ready to act upon doing what's necessary to live a godly life. Instead of worshipping God alone, they tried to blend God worship and Baal worship and it doesn't work that way in God. *You can't find God by fulfilling the sins of your flesh.*

Do you know of anyone who is double minded? A double minded person is easy to recognize because they are often restless and confused in their actions, behavior, and thoughts. They are usually upset with themselves over the small things and they are generally in conflict with themselves. Their inner conflict stops them from leaning on God and His promises.

Some paint a picture of a person who's double minded as a drunk who totters from side to side while trying to walk towards a given destination. This isn't correct. A better visual is a person who walks out of their house to their sidewalk. They are planning on going to the store, so they turn right and walk ten feet and stop. They stop because they think they are *making a mistake* and going the wrong way. So they turn around and walk *twenty* feet. This takes them ten feet past their starting point and they stop again and turn around because they are thinking they made another mistake. Once again they turn and go through this repetitive process of constantly second guessing themselves over and over again.

It's almost like an armed sentry that's standing duty and keeps walking the same path. They continuously walk back and forth, moving but never making progress!

Being double minded is a danger to your mission, purpose, and ministry. James 1:6-8 says, *"But let him ask in faith, with no doubting, for the one who doubts is like a wave of the sea that is driven and tossed by the wind. For that person must not suppose that he will receive anything from the Lord; he is a double-minded man, unstable in all his ways."*

When we become indecisive it allows room for the enemy to work in our lives *against the commands of God.* If we are divided in our interests, or if we are wavering, uncertain, or doubtful, we must learn to go to God in faith and ask Him to teach us to deal with the sin of our doubt because it will hamper our lives and our ministries.

Notice that being double minded is a spiritual condition that operates in every area of our lives. The text says he is unstable in *"all his ways."* This means every facet of his life is under constant scrutiny. *Did I marry the right woman? Should I have married someone else? Maybe I shouldn't have gotten married! I hate my career and all the choices I made since college! I need another job! I should have gone to the Marines instead of going to college! Why, why, why?*

This can get very depressing, and very exhausting! A double-minded person will drive you crazy!

So what's the answer to being double-minded?

How do we kill the message of fear? James tells us it's all about *location, location, location.* James 4:9 says, *"Draw near to God and He will draw near to you. Cleanse your hands, you sinners; and purify your hearts, you double-minded."*

Study Guide

Chapter 5: Walk With Me, Lord!

1. Is there an area of your life that you would describe as a "tedious journey?" Can you share this story? Explain why you feel this area is tiresome or burdensome to your ministry?

2. Describe a time when you had to learn to walk with God? Was this an easy task? Why or why not? Can you share what made you decide to trust God and follow His pathway for your life?

3. Can you share a time when the enemies of God tried to cause you to walk away from Christ? What was it that made you listen to the voice of God rather that walk away from Christ?

4. Think about the one area of your life that you are currently struggling in. Why have you not given this area to God? What is it about this area that has you struggling? Why does God have to allow it to die before you will trust Him?

5. Are there any areas in your life where you could

be considered "double-minded?" Are these issues due to your desire to follow your pathway or His? Double-mindedness is a condition that shows areas where we are not fully convinced of God's grace and power. Can you discuss this with the class?

CHAPTER 6

The Conclusion Of The Matter

When He came into the house, He permitted no one to go in except Peter, James, and John, and the father and mother of the girl. Now all wept and mourned for her; but He said, "Do not weep; she is not dead, but sleeping." And they ridiculed Him, knowing that she was dead. But He put them all outside, took her by the hand and called, saying, "Little girl, arise." Then her spirit returned, and she arose immediately.
~Luke 8:51-55

Celebrate endings - for they precede new beginnings.
~Jonathan Lockwood Huie

As we press towards the conclusion of this book, I would like to spend a few moments talking to you about endings. Everything on this planet has an ending. Every man, woman, boy, or girl will have an ending. This is the way of life. Relationships, friendships, employment opportunities and even pauses have an ending.

This is why Jesus' arrival to Jairus' house is so important. It's not the beginning of life or the race that's most important. It's the end.

Up until this time everything that transpired in Jairus' story was done in the public eye. In the beginning of the book we read when Christ arrived onto the shores there was a multitude of people who were waiting for Him. We see Jairus' first encounter with Christ at the crowded sea shore. We followed them on the pathway to Jairus' home, and we experienced the healing of the woman with the issue of blood, all in the public eye. However, for the resurrection of Jairus' daughter, things moved into a private and more intimate setting, and the actions of Christ speak volumes to us as He made it His purpose to enter Jairus' home.

In this instance the intent of Christ was the same for Zacchaeus and Jairus. His purpose wasn't just to save the individual, or simply resurrect Jairus' daughter. We see the main purpose of Jesus was to bring salvation to the entire household.

If there is any place Christ desires to abide, it's in the homes of His children. If you look again at the story of Zacchaeus in Luke 19: 1-10, you'll see this principle stands out in Christ's address to Zacchaeus. At the beginning of the conversation Christ told Zacchaeus *"Today I must stay at your house";* however, at the end of the conversation *and after Zacchaeus had repented of his illicit business dealings,* Christ said, *"Today salvation has come into this house!"*

So what did Christ find when he entered Jairus' home? First, he found a home with no spiritual structure. How can a house be a spiritual home when Jesus isn't the center of it? As Jairus was a synagogue official, they carried all the airs of being spiritually strong; but with the death of his daughter, Jairus' house was exposed for what it was. It was an empty house that carried only the pretenses of God. *Like a house with unopened Bible lying on a coffee table.*

You might think this is absolutely the wrong place for a basketball terminology, but I believe it is fitting in dealing with endings. When Christ entered the house he told the mourners, *"Do not weep; she is not dead, but sleeping."* In basketball terminology this is what's known as a *"check!"*

On many basketball courts when games are being played, you will often here the phrase "CHECK!" yelled loudly and clearly to players on the court. The phrase can be said by the defense or the offense *during an intermission right before the game resumes*, in an attempt to make sure the participants in the game where ready to continue.

In this moment His statement to these mourners was a spiritual *"check."* Christ was seeking to determine if they had enough faith to witness this miraculous healing. Sadly, instead of receiving the words of Christ in faith, they ridiculed Him which led Him to removing them from the house causing them to miss the blessedness of her resurrection.

So why did Christ remove this group of mourners? I believe he was removing everyone in the house who possessed the wrong spirit.

Usually people who have been on pause for a long time develop a "living in a bubble perspective" because they believe life is passing them by. When a person develops this attitude they regress from the public and become more self-focused. It's almost as if their "bubble" is the circumference of living, and they view themselves inside with their issues of pause and everyone and everything else is outside. When they think of themselves, they think that their opportunities and life are passing them by while life is going full speed ahead for everyone else.

This is the danger of allowing professional mourners (Amos5:16, Jeremiah 9:17) inside your spiritual house! When you add your "bubble perspective" and their "professional mourning" inside of your spiritual home, it compounds the situation and traps you in circumference of pain and negativity. So what's the purpose of professional mourners? They seek to keep you trapped in whatever mournful situation you find yourself in!

It's hard to stand in faith when you are constantly surrounded by lookie-looers and professional mourners. When you are on pause in an area of your life, the only people you need in your bubble are people who will help you find the restoration you need to get off pause. See professional mourners are people who love to put all their energy and efforts into crying over things that are dead. Christ comes to bring life. So the removal of these people was necessary so that Jairus and his wife could move in faith.

Professional mourners are people who get paid to lament or mourn over the passing of a person. In a natural sense they are people who can't get past losing a particular job, or a particular girlfriend. These people often seek to remain in the mournful moment, and they choose to remain stuck while Christ seeks to bring them out of their situation. If you've never seen a professional mourner, they are easy to spot because they constantly perform three main distracting tasks. They cry over every drop of spilled milk. Believe in personal disfigurement (2 Samuel 3:31, Job 2:13), meaning during the mourning process they will not take care of their physical needs. They will not bathe or dress appropriately, and they always look down or sad. This is often practiced so you can see them in their mournful state and cater to their excited and often exaggerated condition. Then they wail loudly seeking to make a spectacle of themselves so they can show how much the person or situation meant to them. (Exodus 12:30, Ecclesiastes 12:5).

Everyone in the house, as well as the local community, already knew of the death of Jairus' Daughter. For many of them it would have been natural for them to come to the house to mourn for her departed soul. However, Christ did not come to attend a funeral; He came to renew life. Since their spirits weren't operating in faith, He had them removed from the premises. Sooner or later we must learn to remove our "mourners" that only want to grieve over the dead or lost things in our lives.

Could Christ still operate in faith and resurrect the dead girl? Absolutely! However, Christ did not send the mourners out of the house because He could not do what was necessary to bring this child back to life. He did this for Jairus and His wife.

My Valley Of Dry Bones

I would like to share with you a recent revelation

of the spirit God has given to me. We all have a valley of *dry bones*. None are exempt. This valley can be found in the book of Ezekiel 37: 1-17. This is the area of our spirits where our "pauses" go to die. This is the area where our hopes, dreams, and aspirations lie dead and dormant like the body of this child separated in another part of the house.

Yes, you know this area of your life is dead, but you feel as long as it's in another room you can go on living without having to pay it too much attention. Since we feel God isn't moving fast enough or we've waited so long for the miracle to happen, we simply let go of the thing we believe God for and we allow them to ultimately die.

If you have allowed some part of your life to die while you were on pause, keep in mind it doesn't have to stay dead. Remember Christ has resurrection power. In a spiritual sense Jairus' daughter's death was a valley of dry bones.

As you are reading this book, I must ask, "*Are there any areas of your life that have been on pause for so long you chose to let them die?*" Did you just walk away from God saying, "*It's dead. It's over. It will never come back alive.*" If so, I say to you *stop believing the enemy!* Death and sleep are the same in God as both words are simply used to describe a person who's temporarily in an unconscious state. Christ told his disciples that "*Lazarus sleeps.*" Although his body had been in the ground for four days he was still resurrected, so why should Jairus' daughter be any different? *Why should your hopes and dreams be any different?* If Jesus can resurrect this dead and dormant army in Ezekiel 37 and say to them, *"get up and shake the dust from your bones,"* why can't He do the same thing for you?

Jesus wants your dry bones to live again, but do you have the faith to believe God? Remember, just because you've failed, it doesn't make you a failure! Some hopes and dreams just need Jesus to pay the house a visit and they can be resurrected.

Keep in mind God can resurrect any aspect of your life, but there is a twist. This time you have to speak to your bones! Maybe it's your marriage. Maybe it's your relationship. Maybe it's your pursuit of your college degree. Either way it can be resurrected in Jesus' Name if you follow His word and stand in faith while you speak to your bones.

I find it ironic that before God raised these dead bones, He made Ezekiel walk among them. This made Ezekiel do two things: first, it made him take notice of *how many bones* were in the valley and the *condition of the bones* in the valley. When God calls us to look in our valley, He wants us to take stock of the blessings, dreams, and testimonies that we have allowed to die because we turned away from Him. How many relationships are suffering because we turned away?

Also I found it surprising that when God began to discuss the situation of the bones with Ezekiel He did not speak to the bones directly. God commands Ezekiel to speak in His name. The question of "Can these bones live?" is a question only God can answer, and it is best left to ask, instead of tell. Ezekiel knew God could raise the dead but he left that decision up to Christ. So to see the bones live we must know we have to go to God in prayer. Remember he is our source. God does not speak to the bones. You must learn to utilize the spiritual authority God has given you. Remember we *"do not wrestle against flesh and blood, but against principalities, against powers, against the rulers of the darkness of this age, against spiritual hosts of wickedness in the Heavenly places (Ephesians 6:12).* You have to speak it in the spirit and allow the power of God to flow through you. This takes time with God in prayer.

Next, God proves to us that even when it comes to miracles and healings, He is still a God of order and structure. Notice the process of healing started with the bones, but it continued until the whole body was raised up and able to stand on its feet. *"The bones come together, bone to its bone" (v. 7), "flesh grew" and "skin covered them" (v. 8), "breath entered them,"* and *"they stood up" (v. 10).* First Ezekiel heard the rattling and then the saw the sinew come up on the body. Even though the bones were dry they still heard the word of God spoken through Ezekiel. This lets us know that no matter how far away with get from God He can still reach us, if we allow Him to. God shows us there are two separate acts in bringing this army back to life. There is the physical act and the spiritual act.

Sometimes in our lives we get dried up. Pauses in life can do that to you, but we must always remember our pauses in life are temporary. They were never to be permanent. We shouldn't have areas of dry bones but many of us do. It is my belief that we can resuscitate these areas and allow them to come back to life.

You might be curious as to why I am discussing the resurrecting of these "dry bones." Think back to Chapter Five where I shared how I had to learn to walk differently, and in discovering to walk differently I had to speak to my leg.

See the nerve I damaged is called the peroneal nerve, and its function is to allow you to raise your foot upwards and turn your foot outwards. As this nerve was "dead," I underwent a new surgery. The doctors removed the tendon that allows a person to turn his foot inward, transferred and placed it on top of my foot.

Now please don't let me lose you. The doctors moved the tendon that would turn my foot inward, which controlled twenty percent usage of my foot, and placed it on top of my foot giving me sixty percent usage. So simply put, they moved the location of one tendon, and by doing that it allowed me greater movement and freedom in that area of my body

After the tendon had healed and the doctors removed the cast, I remember sitting at home one day looking at my leg and praying. I had a hard time trying to rehab it and things just weren't going well. It was then that I cried out to God, and He took me to Ezekiel 37 and said, *"Ray, you gotta speak to your leg."*

At first I did not understand because I was looking at my leg in the natural sense when God was commanding me to look at it in the spiritual sense. All I saw was damaged sinew and flesh when I looked, and God said, *"Yes it is physical but your issue is spiritual. You need to speak to your leg in the spirit. Lay hands on your own leg and you will recover. Your will plus the authority I give you in this area are enough to make your leg respond and grow strong."*

So I laid hands on my leg and started to pray! Lord, did I ever! I declared its healing in Jesus' name. I spoke to my leg, I laid hands on it, and I prophesied to it. After that prayer I went right back to my rehab. Now my full healing did not happen overnight. There were still rough days ahead, but little by little my leg started to respond to the impulses from my brain, and before I knew it I was up walking again.

Yes, in a way we all are like Jacob. We all have areas of our lives where we walk with a limp.

On a personal note, I might not be able to run as fast as I once did, nor can I jump as high, but praise God I can run and I can jump. I had to learn to speak to my bones to obtain my healing

You might be reading this book right now and you're tottering. You want to speak to your bones but you just don't know how. Well my prayer is you will first go to God to ask permission to speak to your bones. This is not done because you don't trust God, but as you are about to try to access God's power, it is just right you ask for His permission.

Now some think God is a "genie in a bottle" and He is just around to serve our every wish and desire. This is not true. *Our God is God and we must seek to serve His will. He does not seek to serve ours!* I was only able to prophesy my healing *because God said so.* If He didn't give me *approval* my words would have been dead prayer because He wouldn't hear it.

Which brings about a question? Why must the treasures and most precious gifts we love be taken away from us before we get our minds centered on God? One of my favorite scriptures deals precisely with this issue. In I Samuel 30:8 David had left Israel, submitted himself under heathen leadership, was about to fight against the people God had selected him to lead, and then God allowed the enemy to come in and steal his most prized possession, his family.

This brought David back to his senses! When God wants to get your attention He will allow the devil to touch the things you love. By God allowing the Amalekites to steal David's treasure, it caused him to refocus on God and find himself.

Now here is the truly blessed part of this text. The Bible says his men desired to kill him but David encouraged himself in the Lord. Instead of David gathering his men and saying, "*Let's go get our women,*" he went and had a talk with the Lord. The text says, "So David inquired of the Lord, saying, "Shall I pursue this troop? Shall I overtake them?" And He answered him, 'Pursue, for you shall surely overtake them and without fail recover all.'"

David's family was the most important thing to him, and I'm sure he was a bag of nerves, but he *still* waited to get the right answer from God. Will you wait to get the right answer from God? Or will you try to tell God what He's going to do for you? Because once God has our full attention, He begins to "press play" in our lives.

Press Play

Imagine you've just had a *very* bad day! Someone hit your car in the parking lot, they are laying off at your job; and to top it off, you lost your keys to your house! After all that drama and heartache you finally make it home, grab your CD player, and you press play! A few seconds pass, then you hear the sound of the artist's soothing voice, and instantly you begin feeling better. Soon a smile comes across your face, your spirits get lifted, and before you know it you've forgotten all about your cares and issues of the day.

The more you listen to the CD the better you feel, and before long you are singing along with the music praising God for the things that happened during the day. You begin thanking God that you are covered by your insurance and no one was injured when your car was hit. You praise God that your résumé is updated and you have interviews next week. You also praise God you had a spare set of keys in the garage!

Now to think, the change in your day began because you pressed play.

Well my friend, when God presses play in our lives immediately things begin to change. Like the CD, when we are paused, we can't move. We are stuck and we feel trapped in a glass bubble. We can't do the things God has intended for us to do because we are stationary. However, when He presses play it puts us in motion, and we are able to complete whatever assignments He has placed in our paths.

As I said earlier we all have dry bones in our lives that we need Christ to press play. Maybe your valley of dry bones is your marriage, or maybe it's your relationship with your family. Either way you have to give God access to your valley and allow Him to bring those dead bones back to life.

All It Takes Is A Word From the Lord

Pauses are God's way of teaching us to trust, wait, and depend on Him as He guides us throughout our daily living. Sure, they are not fun, nor do they feel good as we are going through the trials we face on a daily basis. Since pauses teach us that it's not about our will but His, they are necessary for us to learn that He is the directing force of our lives.

This is why we must celebrate our endings because they lead us into a new beginning. Remember the word Jairus received from his servant? He was told that his daughter was dead. This is something that Jairus could not control, so to have any hope of ever seeing his daughter resurrected, his only recourse was to commit his entire being over to Christ.

In knowing this we can see that her death brought the faith of her father to life in Jesus Christ.

With the issues you are facing in life this might be a constant struggle. You are stuck on pause and you have no idea how to come out of your bubble. However God does, and He has a word that's tailor made for your situation just as He had one for this dead child lying in the bed at her father's house. Keep in mind no matter how dire or dark the situation is all you have to do if pursue Christ, allow Him total control, and give Him permission to speak a word into your situation to make every dead area to come alive.

Study Guide

Chapter 6: The Conclusion Of The Matter

1. If Christ entered your physical house what would He find? Would he find a spiritual house that is built on His teaching? Or would He need to clean out the mourners that are hindrances to your blessing?

2. As you think back over your life what hopes, dreams, and aspirations are you carrying around with you that have died because you feel it took too long for Jesus to arrive? If you know that Jesus has resurrection power, can you take Jesus to these areas and ask Him to resurrect them?

3. Are you ready to lay hands on your dry bones? Why or why not? God has given you the power to resurrect these areas in Jesus' Name, so don't wait any longer; begin to talk and walk in faith as you declare the word of God into your spiritual pause.

4. As you begin to press play in your life how do you

feel about your pauses? Do you see them now as a help or a hindrance to your walk in Christ? Were they a burden or a blessing?

Conclusion

Thank you for taking this journey with me.

What you have read in the preceding pages is what God gave to me in my personal life.

They are steps that I had to take to learn the "why" of my life and the reasons why the Lord chose such a worthless case to use in sharing His name.

As I am still a work on His wheel, in the most humble spirit, I thank Him for all of His blessing and I thank Him for every day of my life.

Child of God, God's Will is perfect! You may have gone through some very rough times in your life, but God brought you through. Now, He wants to use your life for His purpose.

I pray that you will let Him in.

Father, I ask right now, that You touch my friend reading this book. I pray that You will show them that everything that has happened in their lives has been inside Your Will. I know they might be hurt and damaged, but I ask You to give them the strength to climb on Your wheel and be re-created in your likeness. I pray that You will bless them, sanctify them for Your purpose, and use them to be a light in this world. I thank You for each and every one who will call on the Name of The Lord and I pray that You will lead and guide them into a better revelation of Who and What You are to them. In Jesus' name, Amen.

Decision for Christ

For The Unsaved:

The decision to accept Jesus Christ as your Lord and Savior is the most important decision you will ever make. You'll experience purpose, peace, joy, and a secured eternity in Heaven through your relationship with Christ. Pray this prayer and accept Christ as your Lord and Savior.

"Heavenly Father, Your Word says that 'if I believe in my heart and confess with my mouth that Jesus Christ is the son of God I will be saved.' Father, I am a sinner. But I believe in Jesus Christ as my savior. I believe that Jesus died to pay for my sins and then rose from the grave for me. I accept you into my life. I turn from doing things my way. I give you total control of my life as I submit my will to Yours. Thank you for saving me and giving me new life. Amen."

Contact Us

If you would like to contact us please write to us at:

Dr. Rayford E. Malone Ministries
P.O. Box 10135
Dothan, Alabama 36304

Or email us at: remm@rayfordemalone.org
Our Website: www.rayfordemalone.org

Also Available from Rayford Malone

Co-Authored

www.ingramcontent.com/pod-product-compliance
Lightning Source LLC
LaVergne TN
LVHW051557070426
835507LV00021B/2626